With *Streetwise Spirituality,* Jim Thomas continues to answer real human needs with real-life theology. I cannot recommend his insightful writing too highly. Read it and then buy a copy for a friend. Good stories are always meant to be passed on.

—CHARLIE PEACOCK
musician and author of *At the Crossroads*

Where the rubber hits the road is where the Word hits the world. *Streetwise Spirituality* filled my tank and increased my traction for evangelism on the highways, byways, and cyberways of postmodern living.

—LEONARD SWEET
author of *SoulTsunami and Faithquakes*

I've been saying for several years that I wish there were a basic introduction to spiritual growth that I could give my friends who are new to the Christian faith...a contemporary book that sparkles with clear, understandable language...that doesn't go on any sidetracks theologically...that is simple without being simplistic...that is intelligent without being over people's heads...and that inspires as well as informs.

Well, Jim Thomas has written that book. *Streetwise Spirituality* fills a real need, and I'll be buying and giving away a lot of copies!

—BRIAN MCLAREN
pastor of Cedar Ridge Community Church,
Spencerville, Maryland,
and author of *Finding Faith*

Jim helps us base our beliefs on well-developed theological frameworks that bear up under logical examination. He assists us in knowing not just what we believe, but why.

—PHILIP D. DOUGLASS, PH.D.
Chairman, Practical Theology Department,
Covenant Theological Seminary, St. Louis, Missouri

Coffeehouse Theology
by Jim Thomas

Using humor and anecdotes, Jim draws on years
of research and experience to explore Christian
issues and give honest answers to questions that
include: Does God exist? Is doubt a sin? Why is
there suffering?

*Nominated for the Gold Medallion award of the
Evangelical Christian Publishers Association.*

Streetwise Spirituality

Jim Thomas

HARVEST HOUSE PUBLISHERS
Eugene, Oregon 97402

STREETWISE SPIRITUALITY

Copyright © 2001 by Jim Thomas
Published by Harvest House Publishers
Eugene, Oregon 97402

Library of Congress Cataloging-in-Publication Data

Thomas, Jim, 1954–
    Streetwise spirituality / Jim Thomas.
        p. cm.
    Includes bibliographical references.
    ISBN 0-7369-0652-5
        1. Spirituality.   I. Title.
BV4501.2.T455 2001
248—DC21

                                                                                    2001016755

Printed in the United States of America

01   02   03   04   05   06   07   08   / BP-CF /   10   9   8   7   6   5   4   3   2   1

*Celebrity does not always equal significance.
It is certain that the people who make the most noise
and get the most attention in a culture are not always
the most important people within that culture.
They are not always the great philosophers or theologians,
musicians or movie stars, pro athletes or the rich and famous.*

*My mother, Nancy Schell, is a quiet person of strength
and character. She models a consistent faith, a generous heart,
and a steady trust that the Lord has everything under control.
Someday, when I grow up, I want to be just like her.*

Acknowledgments

Thanks to my good friend (who also happens to be my editor) Terry Glaspey. It's nice to have an editor who cares about more than spelling and punctuation. Thanks also to Bob Hawkins Jr., Carolyn McCready, and all the other great folks at Harvest House Publishers who have committed themselves to making a place for books like this one and writers like myself.

Thanks to my agent, Sarah Fortenberry, whose insightful guidance and mature advice keeps the ball rolling.

Thanks to Dallas Willard, Joe Focht, Steve Brown, Chuck Smith, Scotty Smith, Roy Carter, Philip Douglas, Brian McLaren, Robert Benson Jr., John R.W. Stott, and Alister McGrath. How wonderful to see all of your names in the same paragraph! How indelible the impact your thoughts have made on my spiritual life!

Thanks also to my family: Nancy Schell, Rick and Liz Schell, Duane Schell; Larry, Mary, Mary Anne, and Matthew Thomas; Sally Ann Thomas; Sid and Anne Wright; Dan and Melani Bayless; Charles, Heather, and Sydney Davis.

Thanks to my brothers and sisters at Watershed, too numerous to mention, who walk the life of faith with me on a weekly basis. Your friendship has become more precious than I could have imagined.

And as always, thanks to Kim, my best friend and true companion.

Contents

No word has been used to reach absolutely opposite concepts as much as the word "god." Consequently, let us not be confused. There is much "spirituality" about us today that would relate itself to the word god or to the idea god; but this is not what we are talking about. Biblical truth and spirituality is not a relationship to the word god, or to the idea god. It is a relationship to the one who is there, which is an entirely different concept.[1]

Francis Schaeffer

Spirituality and Relationship

EVERY AUTHOR, EVERY SPEAKER, EVERY VENDOR of words, expresses himself from of the well of his own experience. In talking about spirituality, I'm aware there are as many ideas on the subject as there are people willing to talk about it. Each of us has a starting place. This book reflects what I believe to be a biblical model for spirituality, a model rooted in and illuminated by the wisdom of the ancient Scriptures, and understood through my own experiences as I have walked the path of a Christian pilgrim for the past 40 years.

The life of faith can and should include both the intellectual and the experiential. Some people are drawn to one side more than the other. But those who disallow spirituality a rich theological content are vulnerable to embracing a deluded, subjective irrationalism. And those who disallow spirituality a real encounter with the living God are vulnerable to embracing a hollow and wooden religion.

My attempt here has been to find a balance and not travel so far to one side as to risk ignoring the other. Some of you will wish I had focused more on the mystical side, others, more on the theological. I hope that, in spite of any imbalance in what follows, God will use the words you find here to encourage you toward a richer and deeper life with Him.

The context for my own experience began with, and was shaped and molded by, years of mistakenly thinking that spirituality and religion were one and the same thing. They are not. Sadly, our present culture has fostered a spirituality with little religious content and our churches are full of religious people who have as little interest in spirituality. With each passing generation I see a shift in attitude toward a "build-your-own, salad-bar" spirituality that is increasingly person-relative, with far less of a shared, historic foundation. We are quickly becoming a nation of people who are a hundred miles wide but only a quarter of an inch deep because we have so little in common at the center of our souls. Furthermore, as a culture we have replaced the soul with the self, and in so doing, we've become disconnected from each other and disconnected from God.

Fortunately, the inescapable fact is that human beings have been created as spiritual beings. It's part of our hardware. We will always find ourselves, drawn back time and again to search, longing to somehow connect with and live in relationship with God.

In the pages that follow I will explore spirituality from the perspective of the historic Christian faith, the time-tested faith whose God has rescued my heart and renewed my soul. It's the faith I have embraced with my head and that I awkwardly and inconsistently attempt to live out. But Christian spirituality is not so much about religious actions as it is about an active relationship with God. It is for all those who live life unceasingly hungry for more, haunted by an insatiable desire for that which lies beyond the reach of this world. It is for those who are desperate enough, who have exhausted all the possibilities and achievements they can muster on their own, and who are ready to find renewal for their soul and courage for their heart, all in the simple act of surrender to and trust of the God who is there.

- What does the term "spirituality" really mean?

- How does Christian spirituality differ from spirituality in general?

- How can we find fulfillment in our spirituality?

1

What Is Spirituality?

We only know what matter is when spirit dwells in it; we only know what man is when God dwells in him.

William Temple

What Spirituality Is Not

WHEN I FIRST MET MY WIFE, she was 15 and I was 19. We were at a church camp called River Valley Ranch in Millers, Maryland, she as a camper, I as the lifeguard. Now, Kim will tell you that for her, it was love at first sight. No, *really*, you can ask her sometime. However, as has often been the case, I was a little slower to "get the message." We were standing outside the RVR dining hall along with a hundred other sunburned summer campers, anxiously waiting to get in for some of that delicious and always nourishing camp food. Kim (who not only gets the message faster than I do but then goes on to remember minute details surrounding the message longer than I do) tells me I was wearing a trendy pair of brown velvet bell-bottoms, some platform shoes, and a yellow oxford-cloth shirt, and a cleverly coordinated brown velvet bow tie. I know what you're thinking: What girl *wouldn't* fall instantly in love? (A-hem.)

My point here is not how dashing and debonair I was, but that when I was wearing them, bell-bottoms were "in." However, in the 20-plus years since that fateful week at RVR, bell-bottoms have gone in and out of style a couple of times. American culture seems to view clothing and fashion as subject to planned obsolescence. What they told you that you simply must have this year, they tell you that you simply must replace next year. Why? Maybe because we all like new things, but more likely so we can all help whoever "they" are make their condo payments.

It's not just about clothing, though. When I was in high school, "muscle" cars, shag carpet, 8-track tape decks, high-top Converse tennis shoes, the Doobie Brothers, and the Doors were all the rage. (I know, I'm really dating myself here.) Thankfully, things have changed a good bit since then. I for one was glad to see the demise of shag carpeting and 8-tracks.

These days, it seems that spirituality is popular again. Bookstore shelves are packed with the musings of hundreds of would-be spiritual gurus peddling "new improved" brands of spirituality and promising that if you buy their books, attend their seminars and embrace and employ their ideas, you will find spiritual fulfillment. There are as many choices as on the menu of a Chinese restaurant.

Today's spiritualities have some common elements. By and large they are custom-designed to put you in touch with yourself, help you achieve personal happiness, and satisfy your deepest desires for fulfillment. And the wonder of it all is that the new spiritualities ask so very little of you yet promise so much, if you will only take the time to look within yourself to find the answers.

I have to admit I like the way that sounds. It appeals to many sides of my character. I like new approaches, I love the idea of a free ride with no strings attached, and I *really* like focusing on "me." But like most people raised in a capitalistic society, and as a thinking person with the last name Thomas (as in "Doubting" Thomas), I'm inclined to ask a few questions and harbor a few doubts. Where do these new spiritualities really lead us? What ultimate source of truth and life are they trying to connect us to? Can any spirituality that is so unabashedly self-focused ultimately satisfy us?

Ever the consumers, thousands of us buy into the idea that newer always means better and blindly fall in line behind the next pied-piper mystic that comes along. Why is this so? At least in part because we human beings have the true sense that something important is missing in our lives. We honestly desire to know what it is and how we can find it. Most of us have reached the conclusion that there is more to life than the things we can see, taste, touch, smell, and hear. The deluded optimism of the Enlightenment that promised that science and human reason could supply us with the answers to all our deepest questions has now faded, and we are left standing in a silent vacuum, listening to the empty echo of our souls, haunted by the unmet desire to know where we have come from, why we are here, and whether we really have a destiny.

But is our only choice to accept a highly suspect, sloganized, "have it your way" spirituality that's trendy, irrational, and subjective? Are we destined to roam from one shallow spiritual fad to another in an endless cycle of novelty and boredom, always seeking but never finding the real thing?

Counterfeit or Real?

You might have heard the story of the incompetent counterfeiter who spent all day making up some funny money. At the end of the day, it dawned on him that he had mistakenly been printing $15 bills.

He figured the only way he was going to get anything out of this batch of bills would be to find a place where the people weren't too bright and get them to exchange his phony money for real cash.

So he traveled to a small town in the backwoods and went into a little mom-and-pop grocery store. He walked up to the old man behind the counter and asked him, "Do you have change for a $15 bill?"

The old man paused for a second, smiled, and then replied, "I sure do. How would you like that? An eight and a seven or two sixes and a three?"

That old man was much brighter than the counterfeiter thought he would be. He was alert and aware enough to think critically about what was going on, and this kept him from accepting a counterfeit of the real thing. Had he not been alert, just running on automatic pilot through his sometimes boring daily life, he could have been fooled by something that, at a casual glance, looked real but would have cost him in the end.

Spirituality as fad or fashion has led many noncritical thinkers to embrace a counterfeit of the real thing. Today's self-focused spiritualities borrow and use the word *soul* when they really mean *self*. At first glance they look like the real thing, but upon further scrutiny it becomes clear where the emphasis lies. We need to understand that a life centered on the self is a counterfeit that will never be satisfying to the soul. A life that fulfills the soul can only be experienced as that life turns upward toward God and outward toward others.

There is a subtle but significant difference between true spirituality and today's version that focuses on soul massaging and sappy clichés about how "special" we all are. Now don't get me wrong, I do think you're special. And I *know* I am (at least, my mother told me I was). But true spirituality is not just about developing a healthy self-image, losing weight, or improving your inner personal-power skills. True spirituality is about being in a dynamic relationship with God our Creator. It's a fully integrated spiritual life that informs and inspires all other categories of life. True spirituality is not compartmentalized or split off from reality. This is where the Christian faith has much to offer to the discussion of spirituality.

So What *Is* Spirituality?

Do you consider yourself a spiritual person? If so, exactly what does that mean to you?

Different people might answer questions like these in a number of ways. For some, spirituality may be so broad as to include everything from formal religion to massage therapy, astrology, tarot card readings, meditation, wicca, the occult, and back-to-nature movements. A discussion of spirituality might include ideas from Eastern mysticism, New Ageism, and even some of pop psychology's Western optimism. Some would say being a spiritual person just means they believe in God.

Others might not even include the idea of God in their answer. For them, spirituality means something ethereal and impersonal. Some would say that being spiritual means they pray from time to time. (Prayer—that's one of those spiritual buzzwords that has lost its value through counterfeiting. When people say they pray, I always wonder what they mean. Are they communicating with someone who might actually be listening to their prayers, who might care about what is happening in their lives? Or is prayer for them just wishful thinking and sending out "positive thoughts"?)

There are some people who base their idea of spirituality on an experience they had that gave them an acute sense of a supernatural realm, perhaps an encounter with something they perceived to be an angel, a ghost, a spirit, a demon, or some other such thing. They may have played with a Ouija board, sat in on a séance, or called a psychic hotline. Others might say they heard the voice of God or the voice of someone who had died. There are even those who have had "near-death experiences." They may have had some kind of accident or illness that caused their heart to stop beating for a moment or two and during that time they had an "otherworldly" or "out-of-body" experience in which they saw a bright light, walked through a tunnel, or heard a voice from the heavens.

From the perspective of the Christian faith, we shouldn't dismiss these experiences as unreal out of hand. There are many instances in the Bible of encounters between the spiritual and earthly realms. People were visited by angels and tormented by demons. God even opened the mouth of a donkey once so it could speak. Understanding the special circumstances and purposes of these events can be enlightening, but that's not my aim here.

Rather, I believe it would be helpful to drop back a ways from any specific and unusual happenings and ask a few questions about the nature of human beings and spirituality. What is it that makes us capable of experiencing the spiritual aspects of life? What part of the human person is it that can sense something beyond the five physical senses? Is spirituality merely intuition, or is it something deeper and more basic to the kind of beings we are? Is our identity, our personhood, limited to our physical body, or is there an immaterial, or spiritual, aspect to who we are as well?

In the pages that follow, I'd like to discuss spirituality from the perspective of historic Christianity. We'll search the time-tested, ancient Scriptures and the teachings of Jesus for practical help in understanding this mysterious aspect of who and what we are.

Spirituality as a Connection with Someone

In contrast to spirituality as fad and fashion, focused on the self, the historic Christian faith views spirituality as a dynamic relationship in which we commune with God personally, learn to worship God exclusively, and walk in obedience to God with consistency. That kind of relationship stems from a proper understanding of at least three things.

First, Christian spirituality involves an understanding of who God is. This deals with questions such as, Does God really exist? Or is He simply a human idea made up to help us feel better about the afterlife? If He does exist, what is He (or It) like? Is He all-powerful? Is He personal or impersonal? Is He loving? Does He care about what happens to us? Is He fair and just? Is God going to one day judge our thoughts and actions?

Second, Christian spirituality involves an understanding of who we are. This area deals with questions such as, What is the nature of the human person? Are we only a physical body, or do we also have a soul? Are we moral creatures, capable of knowing right from wrong? How are we to experience and express our spirituality? What are ways of nurturing our spiritual lives?

Third, Christian spirituality involves an understanding of the relationship that can exist between God and each of us. This deals with questions such as, Can we know God personally? How can we come into a relationship with Him? If He is holy, how can we ever become acceptable to Him? What spiritual disciplines are involved in nurturing a vital relationship with God?

Religions and philosophies can be differentiated by their beliefs about these three issues. Some worldviews hold that God is personal and intelligent, others believe that He or It is just an impersonal force that animates the universe. Some worldviews teach that human beings are a product of chance in an impersonal universe, others teach that we were created in the image of God. Some worldviews hold that we can draw near to God, others believe we can only fear Him.

Christian spirituality is about both *belief* and *encounter*. In my first book, *Coffeehouse Theology,* I offered a conversational approach to the basics of Christian belief. A discussion about Christian spirituality must begin with the understanding that it is rooted in a historic faith that has substance, which is of great value because it means our spiritual experiences are based in and balanced by what we believe to be true about God, ourselves, and others. The ancient Scriptures serve as the roadmap to get anywhere within the life of the spirit. One of the primary things they show us is that what we believe about God must also be coupled with a personal *encounter* with Him. As one theologian put it

> Mere orthodoxy cannot raise dead bones to life. Only God's breath can do that (Ezekiel 37: 1-14). We have to taste the goodness of the Lord as well as declare it as a fact. God's love must be poured out into our hearts before we can credibly speak of it with our lips.[1]

This book is about the "how" of Christian spirituality, how we can taste of the goodness of the Lord as we experience and express the life of faith. It's about the spiritual attitudes and disciplines that are necessary if you desire to grow spiritually. You don't have to be a Christian to understand some of what I will say here, but I must tell you that you will not fully understand these things until you are looking at them from the inside. If we are to find the answers to life's deepest questions, if we are to find satisfaction for our deepest longings, it will only be when we humble ourselves and allow ourselves to be arrested by something new, which can only be found in something that is quite old.

Historic Christianity offers unique answers to our questions about spirituality, answers that are not just trendy but life-transforming. This is because the Christian faith doesn't just lead us to shallow warm and fuzzy feelings, a personality enhancement program, or a set of lifeless religious practices. The Christian faith leads us to a life-changing encounter with the living God.

Whether you consider yourself a person of faith or not, if you have sensed that there is more to life than you are experiencing, that your life is more than just the random movements of a localized conglomeration of flesh, sinew, and bone, hopelessly roaming a dustball-sized planet in a cold and impersonal universe; if you know in your heart that your life is made up of more than the 98 cents' worth of chemicals your physical body is composed of, then I invite you to explore with me the richness of Christian spirituality.

But let me remind you, this is not about "finding yourself." Christian spirituality is about *being found* and rescued by Someone much bigger than you or me. It's about experiencing the God who is there, the infinite and personal God of all creation. That's why Christian spirituality is so thrilling and inexhaustible. That's why, when we live it out with intention, Christian spirituality is always dynamic and never static.

- Why is it that so many people are unfulfilled in life?

- Is this life all there is?

- We have more wealth, more entertainment and amusement than any other generation. Why are we so dissatisfied with life?

- Is it possible to experience some kind of life that will satisfy us?

2

Longing:
Is this all there is?

Our lifelong nostalgia, our longing to be reunited with something in the universe from which we now feel cut off, to be on the inside of some door which we have always seen from the outside, is no mere neurotic fancy, but the truest index of our real situation.

C.S. Lewis

Life Is like a Jigsaw Puzzle...

HAVE YOU EVER FELT AS THOUGH FINDING FULFILLMENT in life is like trying to assemble a jigsaw puzzle that you can't ever seem to finish because there's always a piece missing? Just when you think you have it about figured out, with the image starting to come into view, one crucial piece is still missing. Did it fall off the table? Was it eaten by the dog? Is someone playing a cruel joke by stealing pieces when you aren't looking? Did someone intentionally package it one piece shy at the factory? Frustrated, you try starting over, thinking next time you'll find the missing piece and complete the puzzle. But to make matters worse, each time you try to put it all together, a different piece comes up missing. Peace, contentment, satisfaction, fulfillment, meaning, purpose—these are just some of the terms we use to describe those missing pieces.

As I travel around the country, I've heard many people express something similar. Their common sentiment is, they feel something is missing in their lives. It's not that they haven't achieved significant goals. It's not that they don't have many of the things they thought they wanted. To the contrary, most people acknowledge that this is a great time to be alive. We are the most affluent generation to ever live. We have more disposable income, more high-tech toys, more varieties of entertainment, more access to information than any other culture before us. On the surface, one would think these things would bring us satisfaction, but somehow they don't. Distraction doesn't do it. Escape leaves us empty. Amusement cycles back around to boredom. Even religion can leave our soul as dry as a desert.

What's worse, many people have just given up. They've come to the sad conclusion they will never be able to find anything that will satisfy them. They live under a dark cloud of despair, and it seems to them there is little hope of finding a way out from under its suffocating shadow.

Is This All There Is?

Have you ever gone through a period of time when you asked yourself the question, Is this all there is? I hope you will find some comfort when I tell you that you're not alone. As a matter of fact, *we* aren't alone. I've felt that way too, and so have millions of others. We come from all walks of life, rich and poor, educated and uneducated, all races, all religions, all ethnic backgrounds. We are not just tortured authors, poets, artists, and musicians who often feel more than their fair share of angst and despair. We are also public speakers, star baseball players, bank presidents, and preachers. "Is this all there is?" is often asked by the most successful, the most wealthy, and the most famous, because they've had a full drink from the well of life, they've tasted all there is of what most of us think might satisfy. But just when they thought they would grasp the golden ring of fulfillment in life, it either slipped through their fingers or crumbled into dust.

A Numbing of the Soul

Every now and then, someone from the celebrity culture gets real enough and honest enough to make an observation that goes against the general worldview of that community. In this excerpt from an interview with actor Brad Pitt in *Rolling Stone* magazine, it's clear that Pitt identifies with the deep longing in the heart of his character "Tyler" from the 1999 movie *Fight Club*. (The "Me" is Chris Heath, who was the interviewer.)

> **Pitt:** The point is, the question has to be asked: "What track are we on?" Tyler starts out in the movie saying, "Man, I know all these things are supposed to seem important to us—the car, the condo, our versions of success—but if that's the case, why is the general feeling out there reflecting more impotence and isolation and desperation and loneliness?" If you ask me, I say, "Toss all this, we gotta find something else." Because all I know is that at this point in time, we are heading for a dead end, a numbing of the soul, a complete atrophy of the spiritual being. And I don't want that.
>
> **Me:** So if we're heading toward this kind of existential dead end in society, what do you think should happen?
>
> **Pitt:** Hey, man, I don't have those answers yet. The emphasis now is on success and personal gain. [Smiles] I'm sitting in it, and I'm telling you, that's not it.

Whether you want to listen to me or not—and I say that to the reader—that's not it.

Me: But, and I'm glad you said it first, people will read your saying that and think...

Pitt: I'm the guy who's got everything. I know. But I'm telling you, once you get everything, then you're just left with yourself. I've said it before and I'll say it again: It doesn't help you sleep any better, and you don't wake up any better because of it. Now, no one's going to want to hear that. I understand it. I'm sorry I'm the guy who's got to say it. But I'm telling you.[1]

It can be fairly claimed that when Brad Pitt did this interview, he already had most of what this world has to offer: good looks, youth, fame, and fortune. Pitt has had opportunities that few people will ever get close to in their entire lives. But he has realized something which is profound. In spite of all his wealth, and success, life has remained unfulfilling because "once you get everything, then you're just left with yourself." Pitt too finds himself wondering if this is all there is.

In *The Pilgrim's Regress*, C.S. Lewis wrote, "What does not satisfy when we find it, was not the thing we were desiring." In other words, many people set out to find satisfaction in things they think hold the key, only to find they have been fooled about which things will truly satisfy their deep desires. We know that becoming a rock star won't be enough. Far too many rock stars have risen to the top professionally, only to crash and burn personally. It's likely that rising to the top of your field won't be enough either. Controlling the lives of your family members won't be enough. Pursuing sexual gratification won't be enough. Being a published author won't be enough. Serving as the pastor of a megachurch won't be enough. This is because our deepest longing is not to be numbered among the privileged, the pleasured, or the powerful. Those are the distractions, the decoys we chase while thinking we are in pursuit of the real thing. It's not that there's anything wrong with those things when they're put in their proper place, it's just that they won't ultimately satisfy our deepest longings.

The principle is that nothing finite will ultimately satisfy the deep yearning in our hearts. Opportunities won't satisfy, pleasure won't satisfy, significance won't satisfy. Even reading a book on the subject of spirituality (this one included) will not satisfy the restlessness and longing that haunts our souls.

What I'm Looking For

Several years back, the band U2 had a worldwide hit song entitled "I Still Haven't Found What I'm Looking For." One of the reasons it was so popular is because it struck a chord in the hearts of many people. The message was basically this: *I've been a lot of places, seen a lot of things, and done a lot of things. But in spite of all that, I feel alienated. Life remains unfulfilling and still seems hopeless. I really want to find what it is that will turn things around for me.* The band came up with a great arrangement, and Bono, the band's vocalist, delivered the message with an honesty and passion that resonates with anyone who has ever felt this deep longing and wondered whether life could somehow become meaningful.

Today, millions of people haven't found what they're looking for either. Worse, many don't even know what the "what" is that they should be looking for. For many, just living everyday life is like stumbling around with a ball and chain tied to their soul. Just getting out of bed stirs up questions like: What's the point? Who cares? Why bother?

The French existentialist philosopher Jean-Paul Sartre once said, "A finite point has no meaning unless it has an infinite reference point." There is a sense in which Christian teaching agrees with Sartre, in that human beings are like a finite point. Our lives are contingent; we are not the source of our own being, and we do not sustain ourselves by our own power. We are dependent on many other things simply to exist, to breathe and eat, let alone to find meaning in life. When we try to find fulfillment in the finite, we're like a dog chasing its tail. Every now and then we'll think we have succeeded in catching it, but we have to bite down pretty hard to keep it, and then all we have achieved is sinking our teeth into our finite selves. Not only is the accomplishment disappointing, but it's likely to leave us in a great deal of pain.

Sartre was right about the meaninglessness of existence for a finite point without an infinite reference point. Sadly, Sartre was an atheist, so he himself recognized no infinite reference point. Life for him was ultimately meaningless and absurd. While we might commend him for his insightful analogy and his brutal honesty, this does not mean we must agree with his conclusion about whether there is an infinite reference point.

The answer to Brad Pitt's longing, the answer to U2's longing, the answer to Sartre's longing, the answer to your longing and my longing is all the same. We are all looking for that something infinite that can serve as a reference point for our finite lives. Is there such an infinite reference point? If so, where can it be found?

Looking for the Infinite Reference Point

There is a village community on the panhandle of Florida called Seaside, which attracts people who enjoy getting away from it all. My wife and I like to go there to reflect, write, and rest. We have a little routine we enjoy, which includes an early-morning walk on the beach followed by a period of sitting under an umbrella in our beach chairs for some reading and quiet. Then around 10 A.M., when the crowd swells, Kim and I head back to our cottage for some writing and more reading, and she might pick up her paintbrush and toy with a visual image or two.

In the late afternoon, after the crowds have had their fill of sand and sun, we gather up our beach chairs and head back down to the shoreline for a walk in the dusk and some sunset reading. It's not unusual for us to be sitting in our chairs, staring into the horizon, as the sun disappears down the western end of the white-sand beach. In the quiet of those moments you can experience something gigantic and truly wonderful. You can look out into the ocean, then look harder and farther out, and still not see the end of it all. Fishing boats shrink to the size of gnats, navy battleships disappear into the vast beyond. I know it's not infinite—the ocean holds just so much water—but there is something immense about it that quiets the human heart and reminds us that there is more.

In addition to the visual feast, I also love the rhythm of the surf on the sand as it rolls in and out; the relentless lumbering of the waves, each one sent from some secret origin to remind us of the beauty and order of the physical universe. I suppose I'm something of a paradox, in that I'm drawn at the same time by both permanence and change. There is something permanent and anchoring about the hugeness of the ocean, but something new and refreshing about each incoming wave.

Sitting by the ocean can give our souls a temporary oasis, a place to rest and settle down. I could speak the same way about other places that move me similarly: Puget Sound in the Pacific Northwest, the island of Kauai, and the Côte d'Azur of southern France.

But as wonderful as it is, even if we moved to Seaside permanently, I would soon discover the deepest longing in my soul coming to the surface again, in the same way the missing puzzle piece makes its absence known. The good things of this world, the ocean, the mountains, the rivers and the valleys, provide us with a resting place that is only temporary. As vast and beautiful as they are, we soon discover they are not the thing we are really looking for. While we can appreciate them, we cannot commune with them. They are simply road signs to point us in the direction of the one thing that will ultimately satisfy our soul's longing. C.S. Lewis comments:

> The books or the music in which we thought the beauty was located will betray us if we trust to them; it was not *in* them, it only comes *through* them, and what came through them was longing. These things—the beauty, the memory of our own past—are good images of what we really desire; but if they are mistaken for the thing itself they turn into dumb idols, breaking the hearts of their worshipers. For they are not the thing itself; they are only the scent of a flower we have not found, the echo of a tune we have not heard, news from a country we have not visited.[2]

One of the wisest men to ever walk the planet was a Jewish monarch named Solomon, who lived about 3000 years ago. Solomon had everything anyone could ever want. He had more riches, pleasure, and power than he could enjoy even if he had lived a hundred lifetimes. But in his old age, as Solomon was reflecting on the course of his life, he became quite melancholy, and it's likely this was when he wrote the book called Ecclesiastes, found in the Old Testament of the Bible.

In Ecclesiastes, Solomon dons the name *Qoheleth*, which is Hebrew for "teacher," and the message he passes on to his student readers comes through loud and clear. More than 30 times he refers to life and its experiences as a cycle of emptiness and "vanity." He reminds us that all pleasure, projects, property, and power are vanity. All human understanding and undertakings are vanity. He views all human tragedy, pain, grief, and suffering as meaningless. From beginning to end, and all the way in between, Solomon came to the conclusion that mankind is powerless and blind, unable to make any sense whatsoever of life. "All is vanity and striving after wind" serves as the repeated summary statement throughout the book.

But there is also some incredible hope to be found in this book. In chapter three, Solomon makes the statement that God has set *eternity* in our hearts. This is an amazing claim because it reveals that although we are finite creatures, God has given us the capacity to connect with the infinite and this is why we all feel such deep-seated longing inside us. As Augustine said, "longing makes the heart deep," and spiritual yearning is born out of the possibility of connecting that God has placed within us. When we find life's finite experiences to be less than satisfying, there is nothing wrong with us. We are just experiencing, indirectly, the awareness of eternity that God has made us with. The great news is that God has much more in store for us than this broken and polluted world will ever be able to provide. "God's beautiful but tantalizing world is too big for us, yet its satisfactions are too small. Since we were made for eternity, the things of time cannot fully and permanently satisfy," remarks Derek Kidner.

I highly recommend you read Ecclesiastes, but please don't read it slowly. Read the entire book in one sitting—or you may find yourself ready to give up on everything! On the surface, the mood is somber. Qoheleth writes viscerally, and if you are given to melancholy, he will take you to the edge of the abyss. But the Teacher doesn't leave us without hope. Toward the end of this powerfully honest book, Solomon draws a contrast between two ways of thinking about life. He calls one "folly" and the other "wisdom," and then moves on to show us which path leads to wisdom. In chapters 10 through 12 he makes a transition from the tough realities of despair to the source of hope, and he shows us where we can look for a solution. If our lives are to have any meaning whatsoever, we will need to live courageously and joyfully, and Solomon tells us this can only happen if we learn to trust, fear, and obey our Creator.

This is the beginning point of Christian spirituality. We must recognize that the longing we feel arises because we live in a finite universe that simply cannot offer the satisfaction we are looking for. This longing is haunting and relentless. It will not be silenced by the noise, busyness, and obsessive productivity of contemporary life. But we are not left without an answer.

Christian spirituality points us to the infinite reference point, and the great news is that this infinite reference point is not a "what" or an "it" —it is a "Who." This infinite reference point, is not an impersonal force or fate, but a God with a face. This is the God who calls us to Himself to be in relationship with Him. When we commune with God, He in return communes with us in a way that the rest of created nature simply cannot. As our Creator, He is able to touch our souls, to speak to us, to satisfy the deep longing that churns in our hearts. And ultimately, God's answer is to move us from longing to belonging.

- Are we all alone in the universe?

- Doesn't everyone belong to God?

- Is being a Christian just about believing certain things or is there more to it than that?

- How can we have a meaningful relationship with God?

3

Belonging:
Am I all alone in the universe?

The greatest honor we can give Almighty God
is to live gladly because of the knowledge of
his love.

Julian of Norwich

Designed for Relationship

I RECENTLY HEARD A REPORT about a middle-aged woman who
jumped out the window of her fourteenth floor apartment.
Just a couple of minutes before her death, a man washing win-
dows on the outside of a nearby building had greeted her, and
they had exchanged smiles. Then when he turned his back, she
jumped.

She left a note in her apartment that read: "I can't endure
one more day of this loneliness. My phone never rings. I never
get letters. I don't have any friends!" Ironically, a neighbor who
lived just across the hall told reporters, "I wish I had known she
felt so lonely. I'm lonesome myself."[1]

Have you ever had a deep feeling of loneliness? Have you ever felt isolated, disconnected, or alienated in life? Psychologists have suggested there is an epidemic of loneliness in our culture. For some reason, more and more people are complaining that they feel estranged and isolated.

Interestingly, we have more and better access to each other than ever before. We have cell phones, videophones, digital pagers, wireless e-mail, and a host of other ways of staying in touch. You'd think we would feel more connected and less lonely now than at any other time in the history of the world. Yet, have you noticed how it can ruin some people's day to come home and find there are no messages on the answering machine? Or when they go on-line and don't hear those three little words "You've got mail"?

Someone has said that loneliness is more than just being alone. There's a cold isolation, a hollow silence in the soul when a person is longing for relationship but has no one to turn to. While many people enjoy seasons of solitude, nobody does well when being alone is his or her only option. Loneliness can suck the life right out of a human soul, because we've been created with personality, and personality thrives on relationships, and without healthy relationships, the human soul languishes.

Contrary to popular myth, loneliness is not reserved for single people. There are many married people who live a lonely existence because their obsession with busyness leaves them with no time to either enjoy the relationships they do have or develop any new ones. Others might have a workaholic spouse or a cold and indifferent one. Lonely people live in any number of settings. They might be in a major metropolitan city, walking the streets daily, surrounded by thousands of people, still feeling left out. They can be sitting in a crowded restaurant, circled about by fellow workers and acquaintances, but still have that gnawing sense that when it gets right down to it, they live a disconnected life.

Loneliness has led many people to depression and some to despair. This is because we measure our lives by the vitality of our relationships. If our relationships are mostly nonexistent or troubled, we are left with hollow hearts. If our relationships are vibrant, our soul can seem full. The condition of our closest relationships will affect us most deeply. When you're at odds with someone you see every day, like a fellow worker, it can be upsetting. But when you're at odds with someone you live with, like your spouse or children, it can be disastrous.

On the most intimate level, in the deepest part of our souls, we are never more alone than when we are at odds with God. Because they are spiritual orphans, those people living without a personal relationship with God struggle with the horrible sense that they are all alone in the universe, with no sense of why they are alive, why they feel left out, or what to do about it all.

The Fuel Our Souls Run On

It is very important for us to evaluate our ideas about God if we are to ever discover a meaningful and fulfilling spiritual life. C.S. Lewis put it this way: "God designed the human machine to run on himself. He himself is the fuel our spirits were designed to burn, or the food our spirits were designed to feed on. There is no other. That is why it is just no good asking God to make us happy in our own way."[2] False ideas about who God is will only take us further down the road to spiritual emptiness, frustration, and disappointment.

In this vein, William Temple commented, "If your conception of God is radically false, then the more devout you are, the worse it will be for you. You are opening your soul to be molded by something base. You had much better be an atheist."[3] And so, if we recognize that we are spiritual beings, if we believe in God and express any kind of devotion to God, it becomes vitally important that we focus our spiritual attention on the God who is really there, rather than on a god we have imagined or come up with on our own.

The God with Personality

Christian spirituality centers on the idea of *belonging* to God, of coming into a deep relationship with the God who is infinite and personal. This would not be possible if God were an impersonal force or fate. In his book *True Spirituality*, Francis Schaeffer confirms that "all the reality of Christianity rests upon the reality of the existence of a personal God." What does Christianity mean when it says that God is personal? It means that God has the quality of being a particular personality, as opposed to being an impersonal energy or life force. God is personal, not in the sense that each of us has our own personal god who exists to serve as our private magic genie, divine puppet, or cosmic concierge, but in that God is who He is. He is not simply who any one of us might understand Him to be. God is not subject to human imagination. Recognizing this changes everything.

God is a being who has intelligence, awareness, and real personality. In the New Testament (Matthew 6:9-13) we find the record of what is commonly called the Lord's Prayer. The first few phrases of this prayer speak loudly and clearly of the personality of God. Jesus said we are to address God as "our Father." This clearly tells us that God has personality. A father is a person and is capable of relationship. We are to say to God our Father, "Hallowed be Your name," implying we worship a God who is a person, who has a name. "Your kingdom come" tells us that this personal God is also the sovereign ruler over His kingdom and can exercise His rule. "Your will be done" tells us that God has a will, therefore He has a mind, an agenda, and is self-determined. This is just one of many examples of how the Christian idea of God embraces the fact that God is personal.

Ownership vs. Relationship

Christian spirituality focuses on the God who has designed and created you and me and everything that exists, and the Scriptures reveal that God has built into our software the capacity to have a relationship with Him. There is a popular notion that says we all belong to God and are all God's children, and in one sense the Bible would agree. Deuteronomy 10:14 tells us, "to the LORD your God *belong* the heavens, even the highest heavens, the earth and everything in it" (NIV). That pretty much covers all of creation.

Since God has made everything that exists, everything does belong to God. But this is belonging primarily in terms of ownership. Christian spirituality carries with it the idea that God has offered us the opportunity to move from ownership to relationship. My wife and I love each other dearly, even to the point of saying we belong to each other. But ours is not a belonging of ownership. It is a belonging of relationship, of devotion, of willful commitment and deep trust. Because we have come into this deeply intimate relationship, we have moved from loneliness and longing to belonging on a human level.

When we turn to the issue of spirituality, how do we come into that kind of intimate relationship with God? How do we move from mere existence and ownership to a thriving and personal relationship? Can a person move from his or her deep spiritual longing for God to fully belonging to God? The Christian idea of spirituality says "yes."

Dealing with the Separation

The Christian faith teaches that we are all sinners, and therefore we are all separated from God. This separation is at the root of our sense that something is missing. It is why we are haunted by such a deep longing. It is why we ask the question "Is this all there is?" We feel separated from the very source of life because our sin has put up a barrier between us and God.

Whether or not we know it, what we all long for is to be back in a right relationship with God. While this separation from Him is real, the Scriptures also teach us that God has graciously made a way to bridge the gap that separates us from Him. Christ came and paid the price to ransom us from sin, and because of His death on the cross that ransoms us, when we place our trust in Him the separation between us and God is removed. God didn't owe it to us to make a way for us to come back to Him. It is not something we deserve in any way at all. God has simply done it, and the Bible tells us that the reason God did it was because of His immense love for us.

Our part in dealing with the separation is to respond by recognizing our need for God and His free gift of salvation, and to turn from our sin and bow before Him. We can't work our way into heaven or into God's good graces. His forgiveness cannot be achieved, it must simply be received. We can't tip the balance of the moral scales in our own favor. None of us are good enough for that. The only way to deal with our sin is for it to be forgiven. We begin by admitting our spiritual bankruptcy and powerlessness. We cry out for God's help, and the Bible tells us that all who call on the name of the Lord will be saved. Realizing that you cannot save yourself and placing your trust in Christ, who died for your sin, is the starting point of a life of Christian spirituality.

From Longing to Belonging

When you become a Christian, you take the first step to achieving true spiritual satisfaction because at that point, God moves you from your place of longing to a place of belonging. You move from being alone with yourself in the universe to having a relationship with the infinite, personal God.

There are many concepts of spirituality that take a completely different route to an altogether different destination.

They will sometimes borrow Christian terms, but they actually mean nothing by them. The word "god" or the word "faith" can be superficial or nebulous when employed simply to give a gloss of religious legitimacy to what is in reality empty rhetoric. In the end, if a concept of God or spirituality leads people back around to themselves, or to an impersonal or vague concept of God, it will eventually leave them empty and wanting more. The self can never fill the soul. It is in God alone that we find the answer to our soul's longing. Augustine put it this way: "You [God] have made us for yourself, and our hearts will be restless until we find our rest in you."

The truth and reality of Christian spirituality give your existence meaning because they declare that your life is about more than just you, or the things you own and the things you do. Once you are a Christian, you belong to the God who is a Someone. You belong in a deep and intimate way, not just by ownership but by relationship. Christian spirituality is not just about church attendance or membership, it's about citizenship in a heavenly kingdom and being in relationship with the heavenly King. Once you become a Christian, you are transferred from the kingdom of self to the kingdom of God, from the kingdom of darkness to the kingdom of light.

And there's more good news: It's not based on your performance. You can't move from longing to belonging by being good enough, by praying long enough, by going to church enough, or by doing (or not doing) anything enough. It's only by God's gift that we can enter into this relationship with Him. We put our trust in Christ, we trust that what He did when He died on the cross was enough to bring us back to God, and then God moves us from mere ownership to personal relationship. God has taken the initiative, and now we can not only know *about* Him, but we can actually *know* Him.

The first time a person becomes truly aware of this, it's as if a light goes on inside, and all of a sudden everything in life looks different. As the old hymn says, "I once was lost, but now am found, was blind, but now I see." To many people God reveals Himself in a subtle and most intimate way, and they are drawn into an initial encounter with Him. God may arrange that they encounter Him during some pleasant experience, while down at the beach, up on a mountain, riding a bike, or walking in a garden. Others have found themselves in a situation where they have come to the end of their rope, run out of their own self-sufficiency; and recognizing their need, they desperately turn to God, only to find that He was already there, waiting for them, arranging the whole thing so they would meet Him personally.

God comes and reveals Himself to a person in as many ways as we might be able to imagine. In each case, the encounter is authored by Him, and as Brennan Manning has said, it is then we are "seized by the power of a great affection." The strong grip of God's love and grace brings us into the most secure form of belonging possible, because God has promised that He will never leave us or forsake us.

A Growing Knowledge of God

Belonging to God also includes the idea of our having a hunger to grow in our knowledge of Him. Once we have come to know the Lord, we are naturally interested in getting to know Him better. That is the way it is with anyone that you truly like or love. You want to spend time with them, you want to get to know them better. How can we do this? God has revealed Himself through the written word of the Scriptures and through Jesus Christ the living Word, who became a human being. We can begin to search the Scriptures and find out what God is like, what pleases Him, and how He wants us to live out our relationship with Him. We can also look at the life of Jesus and learn about God in a more direct way. What did Jesus think about love, poverty, wealth, marriage, and telling the truth? What did

Jesus think about holiness and hypocrisy? The answer to these questions is found in the New Testament, which makes available to us a credible knowledge of God.

This always-growing knowledge of God deepens our sense of belonging and provides us with an anchor for our life of faith. Christians believe in God, but we also believe some very specific things about God and about the relationship between God, humanity, and the rest of creation. These beliefs have been summarized in the historic creeds of the church. (For a closer look at the oldest and most widely accepted statement of Christian belief, the Apostles' Creed, see the chapter entitled "What is Christian Faith?" in my book *Coffeehouse Theology*.) These beliefs are foundational and they nurture a steadfast, growing faith.

But belonging to God is not just a matter of head knowledge. It also includes a relationship with Him that we experience from day to day as we respond to Him: worshiping, obeying, and serving from a heart filled with gratitude for what He has given us. It's not just about the initial step of getting "saved." As Dallas Willard has pointed out, following Jesus is not just about "sin management." It's not just about securing our eternal life insurance or having our sin dealt with on the legal and eternal end of things. Although those things are important and are the beginning point, we are also called to become *disciples* of Jesus Christ. We are called to follow Christ, to walk in a daily relationship with God by the power of the Holy Spirit, who lives in every believer.

The Scriptures describe our spiritual belonging as experiential. First Peter 2:9 (NIV) tells us, "You are a chosen people, a royal priesthood, a holy nation, a people belonging to God, that you may declare the praises of him who called you out of darkness into his wonderful light." Jesus says (in John 8:47), "He who belongs to God hears what God says. The reason you do not hear is that you do not belong to God" (NIV).

If you write and teach about theology, as I do, it's sometimes easy to forget the importance of belonging. But we must not reduce our study of God to a scientific system or a ritualized religion. God is not some*thing* we study, He is Some*one* we are in relationship with. God is Someone who loves us and Someone we can express love back to. God has made it possible for you and me to *belong* to Him, as far more than mere possessions. In the deepest part of our souls, there is an empty place that can only be filled when we realize that we belong to God and then go about living in a personal relationship with Him. Belonging to God in this way is the answer to our deepest longing.

In his classic book *The Pursuit of God*, A.W. Tozer sums it up concisely:

> When religion has said its last word, there is little that we need other than God Himself. The evil habit of seeking God-*and* effectively prevents us from finding God in full revelation. In the "and" lies our great woe. If we omit the "and," we shall soon find God, and in Him we shall find that for which we have all our lives been secretly longing.[4]

- How dependent are we on God?

- How far does God go in arranging the circumstances of our lives?

- Isn't God too busy with "big" things? How can He have time to deal with the problems in my little life?

- How can we learn to find our rest in God?

4

Resting:

Leaning into the providence of God

Only afterwards, as we look back over the way we have come and reconsider certain important moments in our lives in the light of all that has followed them, or when we survey the whole progress of our lives, do we experience the feeling of having been led without knowing it, the feeling that God has mysteriously guided us.[1]

Paul Tournier

SHE CRUMPLED TO THE GROUND, TEARS FLOWING, crying out with a moan that revealed a soul filled with anguish and unrest. Hopelessness, fear, and confusion came to the fore and declared victory over the tattered spirit of our young friend.

She was one of the walking wounded, the ones who have been knocked down and feel forgotten, the ones who have lost their spiritual moorings and have slid into the dark abyss of despair. The enemy of our souls thought he had her. It was as if he were already celebrating what he thought was another victory.

She was one of those shy lambs who get isolated and then stray away. Distracted and deceived, she had bought a bag full of lies about whether her life mattered. The circumstantial evidence was in: She was a failure, her life was worthless. There was no reason to get out of bed, no reason to even be alive. The struggle simply wasn't worth it.

But just before the darkness closed in to finally drown out her spirit, she heard a faint voice in the distance. She knew the voice, it was the voice of the Good Shepherd. He was calling out her name. He had missed her. He had gone out of His way, He had come searching to find her again. He had not forgotten her. He lifted her up in His arms, placed her weary body across His shoulders, and spoke these gentle words of comfort:

> Come to Me, all who are weary and heavy-laden, and I will give you rest. Take My yoke upon you and learn from Me, for I am gentle and humble in heart, and you will find rest for your souls. For My yoke is easy and My burden is light (Matthew 11:28-30).

Rest—what a beautiful word. Rest.

Sadly, true rest can be an elusive experience. I'm not talking about getting a good night's sleep or taking a nap, I'm talking about true rest. I'm not talking about taking a vacation or having a long weekend off, I'm talking about finding rest for your soul, the kind of rest that runs so deep that it isn't broken by the demands of everyday life.

Is It Reasonable to Think We Can Find Rest?

> ...And for the support of this Declaration, *with a firm reliance on the protection of Divine Providence,* we mutually pledge to each other our Lives, our Fortunes and our sacred Honor (emphasis added).

After this final sentence from the Declaration of Independence, there are 56 signatures from a rather impressive group of people, including Thomas Jefferson, Benjamin Franklin, and John Adams. What do you suppose they and the other representatives of the 13 colonies meant when they said "...with a firm reliance on the protection of Divine Providence?" What role did the Founding Fathers see divine providence playing in their lives, fortunes, and sacred honor? As they separated themselves from the sovereignty of England, in what way did they see themselves still responsible to a sovereign God, and therefore dependent on His care and guidance in the affairs of their lives as individuals and as a nation?

I suppose the answer is the same one that most people in the United States might give today. By and large, most Americans acknowledge the existence of God and believe that He is "watching over" us in some way. Many find a great deal of rest for their souls and minds in knowing that God is in charge.

Webster defines providence as "the care and benevolent guidance of God." But we might well ask, is resting in divine providence warranted? Does God really watch over us? Is there some reason to believe that the God of the universe has the time and inclination to become involved in our little lives?

Different Views of Providence

As far back as recorded human thought goes, there has always been some kind of belief in divine providence. The idea was summarized early on by Cicero: "That all things, all events in this world, are under the management of God." However, there have been conflicting views as to how much of a "hands-on" manager God is, and not a few of these views have taken some rather extreme positions.

At one end of the spectrum there are those who have thought God takes a "Don't call me, I'll call you" approach.

Under this view, perhaps best known through the religious system called *deism*, God created the world, drop-kicked it over the back fence of the universe, and then stepped back to let things fall where they will. The deistic God is an absentee deity who only becomes involved in large-scale, history-shaping events of His choosing. Being among some six billion individuals living on this tiny, gnat-sized planet we call "Earth," frankly, you and I just aren't that significant. So addressing this kind of God with our prayers is an exercise in futility. We are cosmic castaways, abandoned by our Creator, struggling to survive against the mechanistic laws of a sometimes cruel universe. The deistic God is simply too distant and too distracted to get involved, and as a result, we end up disconnected.

At the other end of the spectrum are those who see God more like the wizard working the controls of the machine behind the curtain. In this view, sometimes called *determinism*, God micromanages every detail of an individual's life. At its most extreme, God is seen as hyperactively involved, controlling every minute aspect of our movements in life, large and small alike. Again, prayer is senseless because God has every detail already planned out. We are reduced to being just another part of the machine, and human free will or choice is practically nonexistent. As a result, we end up in despair.

Another view, more popular in nontheological circles, sees God as the Universal Grandfather in the sky, whose only job is securing the amusement and pseudo-happiness of all His grandchildren. In this self-centered approach, God revolves around our personal dreams, wants, and desires. This subjective view focuses exclusively on one side of God's love and, in effect, reduces God to a cosmic vending machine stocked full with all the things you and I think will make our lives fulfilling. Prayer is more like putting a coin in the machine, pulling the right lever, and expecting God to give us what we want. And, we end up deluded.

Which of these views is true as stated? None. Which represents a balanced and biblical view of God's involvement in our lives? None. Which gives us hope for a dynamic relationship with the living God who is there? None. Why? Because all three of these viewpoints misrepresent God as He has revealed Himself in the Scriptures. The God of the Bible has not left us disconnected, despairing, or deluded.

The error common to all these views is basic, in that they each try very hard to define exactly how God works and how He will always work, and that is simply an impossibility. God will not be tamed by us. God will not be created in our image. God moves and acts as He wills and expresses His love to us as any good parent would, by sometimes giving us the things we desire and sometimes not, by sometimes allowing things to enter our lives that we don't think are so good, and even by allowing us to "fall off our bikes" once in a while. God does all of this because He desires that we come to Him to enter into His rest, to lay our burdens at His feet, to submit our hopes and dreams to His will, and to ask for His guidance and wisdom in every aspect of our lives.

I remember praying about a certain career opportunity that looked very promising. It would have offered me a stimulating new challenge, some needed security, and increased income. But after just a few weeks, the whole thing simply died. My repeated phone calls were not returned. The silence was deafening, and my wife and I were quite frustrated. What was God up to? Why was this happening?

Later, we found out the reason our phone calls weren't returned. The fellow speaking with us had lost his job, and if we had sealed the deal before he had been let go, if we had sold our house and moved, it could have been a very bad situation for us. God knew it wasn't best for us to have this opportunity we thought would be so perfect. God's providence was indeed at work, even though we had gotten so impatient and anxious about the whole thing. We had graciously been given another lesson in learning to rest in His love and care. "Find rest, O my soul, in God alone; my hope comes from him" (Psalm 62:5 NIV).

The Bible's View of Providence

If we are to enter the rest of God's providence, then our discussion should address some of the hard questions: Is God both able and willing to come to our aid? Will God provide for us and protect us? In short, does God truly have our good in mind?

Psalm 119:105 says, "Your Word is a lamp to my feet and a light to my path." This is one of the reasons why it's important for us to explore the depths of the Bible. The Bible is where God has spoken in terms we can understand, and its timeless truths reveal how God, in His providence, responds to our needs.

Throughout its pages the Bible is full of narrative focusing on God's involvement in human history: real stories about real people in real situations. And the Bible isn't just about God's involvement in history on a grand, international scale, but also on the scale of individual human lives.

So what does the Bible say? While we lie awake worrying late at night, tossing and turning, restless and frustrated, is God even aware, does God care? When we need guidance for a decision, will God give it?

If we are to enter into the rest of God's providential care, we must recognize three things: the reign of God, the care of God, and the provision of God.

The Reign of God: God as King of Your Life

The first step to entering into the rest of God's providence in our lives is similar to the first step we take to become a Christian. We must acknowledge the reign of God in our lives. We must come to the place where we admit we are no longer king of our own life. Instead, in trusting abandonment and passionate allegiance, we recognize God as our King. We begin to see ourselves as members of His kingdom, His loyal subjects, and as such, we acknowledge that we belong to God, that we desire to serve, obey, and honor God.

These are noble-sounding words that might conjure up visions of knights and round tables, but what do they mean? I don't know about you, but when I try to think of what they might really mean, I find myself feeling like a pretty lousy subject of the King. But thankfully, as the Bible teaches, being a part of God's kingdom is not about performance, it's about relationship. Christ has purchased us by His blood, and we are His. Our performance will ebb and flow because we are inconsistent in the expression of our love for our King, but relationship is forever. Once we have become one of His, Christ claims us lock, stock, and barrel. Realization of this can be one of the most wonderfully freeing things in the Christian life.

Under God's reign, with grateful hearts we purpose to live our daily lives to honor our King, we spend time expressing our love and allegiance to Him, worshiping Him for who He is and for His love and care in our lives. In our prayers, we lay our burdens at His throne, entrusting to His wisdom everything that we care about. And slowly, over time, we find more and more that we come to care most about the same things our King cares most about.

If we are to enter into the rest of God's providence, it begins with acknowledging the reign of God in our lives. Once we know who our rightful King is, we can find further reason to rest as we discover more about His attitude toward us.

The Care of God: His Eye Is on the Humans Too

As believers in Jesus Christ, we are members of the kingdom of God, and we are under the care of our King, God Himself. This is one of those things that sounds incredibly simple but is so easy to forget. God cares about me. This may strike you as odd, but would you please take just a moment and read this out loud:

God cares about me.

Now, tell the person who just looked at you funny to mind his own business. Say the phrase again three more times, each time placing the emphasis on a different word: first "me," then "cares," then "God."

God cares about me.
God cares *about me.*
God *cares about me.*

Has it sunk in yet? Have you begun to fathom the riches found here? The almighty King of the universe, the God who designed the galaxies, ordered the stars and planets, the omnipotent Ruler of all, cares about you. Not just you in a general "all of humanity" kind of way, but you specifically. *God cares* about *you*.

God's care in our lives can be seen in something Jesus once said:

> Do not be worried about your life, as to what you will eat or what you will drink; nor for your body, as to what you will put on. Is not life more than food, and the body than clothing? Look at the birds of the air, that they do not sow, nor reap nor gather into barns, and yet your heavenly Father feeds them. Are you not worth much more than they? (Matthew 6:25-26).

Notice how in these verses Jesus gives us something to avoid doing, something to do, and a new way of looking at things. In other words, there is a prohibition, a prescription, and a perspective here.

The Prohibition

Jesus begins with "do not be worried." Why would Jesus say that? When He tells us not to allow ourselves to become wrapped up in worry, do you think there is the real possibility that we could live out our lives without suffocating in stress? Is it truly possible to find rest for our soul in God?

My friend Steve Brown tells the story of three men who were arguing over which of their professions was the oldest in history. One was a surgeon, one an engineer, and one a lawyer. The surgeon argued, "It's obvious that I belong to the oldest profession. Remember when God took a rib out of Adam and created Eve? That was surgery, and therefore surgery is the oldest profession!" The engineer spoke next: "No, if you'll go back to the first part of Genesis, you'll find that the entire universe was in chaos and that God created order out of the chaos. That's engineering, and therefore engineering is the oldest profession!" The lawyer, who had listened quietly to each of their claims, smiled for a moment, then stood up and said, "So where do you guys think the chaos came from?"

It's a simple fact that every day the world rolls over on someone who was just sitting on top of it. Just when you think you've got your ducks in a row, one of them drops out, gets run over, or lays a goose egg. Chaos.

It can show up in our lives almost daily. When you're late for work, the phone is ringing, the baby's crying, you haven't paid the mortgage, the car won't start, the auto club is backed up for hours, you spill something on your new suit, and there are dandelions taking over the front yard. Chaos.

Where is God's providence in those times? We cry out in desperation for help, but is God listening? Does God care?

The apostle Paul knew a little bit about chaos. He was shipwrecked, was thrown in prison, and was constantly struggling with what he called "a thorn in the flesh" (probably a physical affliction), and yet through all this chaos Paul echoed Jesus' words, instructing us to "be anxious for nothing, but in everything by prayer and supplication with thanksgiving let your requests be made known to God. And the peace of God, which surpasses all comprehension, will guard your hearts and your minds in Christ Jesus" (Philippians 4:6-8).

According to both Jesus and Paul, while pain is a given in life, misery is optional. The circumstances don't have to rule our hearts and minds. We've got a choice in this. We can turn away from our anxiety and lean hard into God, surrendering to God and receiving His peace as He sends it. When it comes, Paul tells us we won't understand it. It will most likely take us by surprise. Most of us will be found saying, "It isn't like me to be this at ease!" But it *is* just like God. And since we belong to Him and He cares for us, in His providence He graces us with His rest.

Have you ever been worried about something, and later on you looked back and thought: "I can't believe I got so worked up about that! I made a mountain out of a molehill." Is there anything in your life right now that could be like that? Maybe it's a conflict that you fear will come to a head soon. Maybe it's a difficult family member, a noisy neighbor, or a rude coworker, and you're all tied up in knots thinking of how difficult it will be to deal with them. Maybe your life is just too cluttered and your *being* is drowning in *doing*.

Whatever your worry may be stop right now and tell God about it. Be honest, tell Him how anxious you are, tell Him how this is chewing you up. As you are praying, lay your burden down before Him. Leave it there and begin to focus your thoughts off of the problem, away from yourself, and onto the Lord. Don't even think about whether God will change the circumstances, just ask Him to calm the hurricane that is raging in your soul. It might help you to do something physical such as closing your eyes, getting down on your knees, and lifting your hands, palms up towards heaven, as a gesture of openness and submission to God. Then just wait quietly for the Holy Spirit to do His work in your heart and mind. Tell God you want to receive His peace and rest in His love. Lean hard into the grace of God, understand that He cares about you, and find your rest in Him.

The Prescription

In addition to telling us not to be anxious, Jesus gives us a prescription: "Look at the birds of the air, that they do not sow, nor reap nor gather into barns, and yet your heavenly Father feeds them" (verse 26).

What a master teacher Jesus is. Basically He says, "Get your eyes off yourself and focus your attention on an example of God's faithfulness. For instance, look at the birds, and notice how consistently God shows His care for them." God cares for the birds, and you can see it in the fact that they live out their lives one day at a time, without stockpiling massive quantities of food. God shows Himself to be faithful, providing them with just enough for each day.

Jesus wants this everyday example to remind us about something we are prone to forget. God is our Source and has been from the beginning. God created us, designed our stomach with the capacity to feel hunger, our mouth with its capacity to feel thirst. The same God who designed those signals of hunger and thirst has also created a world full of food and water. He has promised to meet our needs for both. The question is whether or not we will trust God to continue being our Source. Jesus says, "Look at the birds, they will remind you of God's faithfulness."

The Perspective

Jesus tells us not to be anxious, urges us to see God's faithfulness, and also gives us a perspective, a little lesson in logic from the author of logic Himself: "Is not life more than food, and the body than clothing?" (Some of you are wondering if this means you have to cancel your subscriptions to *Gourmet*

Cooking and *Vogue*. Although that might be good for some of you, that's not the main point here.)

After clarifying for us that food and clothing do not make up the whole of life, and then pointing out how much God loves our little feathered friends, Jesus makes a statement about the intensity of God's love for us. "Are *you* not worth much more than *they?*" This is an argument from something lesser to something greater, that is, Jesus is saying that, because God cares about the birds, it should be obvious to us that God cares about us also.

Now this may shock some of you, but God is not species-neutral. Though God loves all of His creation and does value birds and take care of them, you and I and all other human beings are the creatures He created in His own image. As such, we are simply more valuable to God than birds, and He will certainly take care of us.

On another occasion, Jesus drove the same point home with a similar analogy:

> Are not two sparrows sold for a cent? And yet not one
> of them will fall to the ground apart from your Father.
> But the very hairs of your head are all numbered. So do
> not fear; you are more valuable than many sparrows
> (Matthew 10:29-31).

There's some amazing information here on how well God keeps track of what's going on in our lives. The word "fall" can also be translated "light," as when a bird alights or lands on the ground. This would mean that God is aware of every move a bird makes, every time it flies and lands.

As far as the verse about the hairs on our heads, there are more than 100,000 hairs on the average human head. The older you get, the more you fall into the Under a Hundred Thousand Club, and some of my friends have even dropped down to the Under a Thousand Club! Whatever the case for you, Jesus says the hairs on your head are numbered. Every single one of them.

I can imagine what some of you must be thinking as you read this. "That's it, Thomas isn't just losing his hair, he's losing his marbles. He's gone off the deep end with this. Jesus was *obviously* speaking in hyperbole. God could not possibly be aware of every bird's launchings and landings or keep track of every hair on every person's head."

I have to admit that those same thoughts occurred to me as well. And it may be true about me and my marbles. But when you start to think about what it means when we say that God is *infinite*, do we have even the vaguest idea of what that could mean? When we say that God couldn't possibly keep track the motions of millions of sparrows, aren't we limiting our concept of God's infinitude? If God really is infinite, then why couldn't He be aware of it if hairs #109, #237 and #34,998 left your head this morning?

When we connect the dots between these images and the truth Jesus was trying to convey, it can set you and me free from worry and anxiety and lead us into His rest. It is the simple understanding that if the infinite God can track billions of bird hops and hair losses, then He can certainly take care of our basic needs.

God keeps track of the hunting of the lion, the flying of the eagle, the spinning of a spider web, and the construction of an ant colony. God oversees the migration of every animal, the motion of every galaxy, and the metamorphosis of every caterpillar into a butterfly.

So, is God watching over you? You bet He is. Does God value you? You bet He does. You can rest in that fact and remind yourself that you are under the care of an infinite, loving, heavenly Father.

The Provision of God: Supplying All Your Needs

Another reason we can find rest in God's providence is His promise of provision. The apostle Paul put it this way: "My

God will supply all your needs according to His riches in glory in Christ Jesus" (Philippians 4:19). That's pretty direct. Paul points us to the person of God, who Himself will be the supply source for meeting our every need.

Notice how David, the great songwriter of the Old Testament, put it:

> *The LORD sustains all who fall*
> *And raises up all who are bowed down.*
> *The eyes of all look to You,*
> *And You give them their food in due time.*
> *You open Your hand*
> *And satisfy the desire of every living thing.*

> Psalm 145:14-16

There is a sense in which we should see everything we have as having come to us through the provision of God. And when it comes to being the source of rest for our souls, the Lord put it in no uncertain terms: "I satisfy the weary ones and refresh everyone who languishes" (Jeremiah 31:25). St. Augustine perceived this clearly in his well-known words: "You have made us for Yourself and our hearts will be restless until they find their rest in You." When we try to fill our hearts with anything that is not God, we will always end up restless. When our hearts learn to see God as the Source of our every need, then we will find true rest.

If we go back to the words of Jesus from Matthew 6, we read (in verses 31–33), "Do not worry then, saying, 'What will we eat?' or 'What will we drink?' or 'What will we wear for clothing?' For the Gentiles eagerly seek all these things; for your heavenly Father knows that you need all these things. But seek first His kingdom and His righteousness, and all these things will be added to you." With promises like these, those who turn to the Lord can have confidence that they will indeed find their rest in Him. He is faithful.

As with many things in life, there is a balance to be sought here. If we thought it were all up to God, we might come to the place where we refuse to apply ourselves in the task of working for those things we need in life. For instance, if you have been praying for God to provide you with a husband or wife, but you never put yourself in the flow of traffic where you will meet new candidates, you may be taking God's provision for granted. If you have been praying for God to provide you with a job, but you aren't out there actively looking for one, you may be taking God's provision for granted.

On the other hand, if we thought it were all up to us, we would be tempted to think of ourselves as self-sufficient. We might set out to grow grass in our yard, read up about the right time and conditions, work hard to aerate, plant the seed, water faithfully, and fertilize etc. And then when the harvest comes, we'd think to ourselves "Ahhhh, look what I have done all by myself!"

We forget that without all that God has done to provide a suitable environment for grass to grow, and all He continues to do in managing His creation, there wouldn't be a single blade of grass in our yard. But because God is generous, He allows us the dignity of participating in the process. God could quite easily have grown the grass without us. And so we work hard, we do our part, but we also get down on our knees, bow before our King, and pray for His continuing provision of rain, sunshine, or whatever else we need.

A little boy was afraid of the dark. One night his mother told him to go out to the back porch and bring back her broom. The little boy turned to his mother and said, "Mama, I don't want to go out there. It's dark."

The mother smiled reassuringly at her son. "You don't have to be afraid of the dark," she explained. "Jesus is out there. He'll look after you and protect you."

The little boy looked at his mother real hard and asked, "Are you *sure* He's out there?"

"Yes, I'm sure. He is everywhere, and He is always ready to help you when you need Him," she said.

The little boy thought about that for a minute and then went to the back door and cracked it open a little. Peering out into the darkness, he called, "Jesus? If you're out there, would you please hand me the broom?"

Jesus doesn't always hand us the broom. Sometimes we do have to go out into the dark and get it. But the little boy's mother was right, we don't need to fear because we are not alone. Jesus has promised that He will never leave us or forsake us.

Resting in God's Providence: Communing with Him

Sometimes confusion and chaos can be the twin thieves of rest. This is why the twin spiritual disciplines of solitude and silence are so important. They require that we stop what we are doing, that we find a place where we can be alone and get still, that we shut out the noise of the world around us and focus our attention on God and on being with Him.

This was important to Jesus too. He used to make a habit out of it. On one occasion, right after Jesus had worked the miracle of feeding a huge crowd with just five loaves of bread and two fish, "He made the disciples get into the boat and go ahead of Him to the other side, while He sent the crowds away. After He had sent the crowds away, He went up on the mountain by Himself to pray; and when it was evening, He was there alone" (Matthew 14:22-23). Notice what Jesus did first? He sent everyone away. He wanted to get alone so He could pray, so He could spend some time with God the Father. And if Jesus needed solitude and silence in His spiritual life, don't you think we do too?

I must admit that this does not come naturally for me. I like to have a constant stream of stimulation going. But as I've begun to immerse myself in these two spiritual disciplines, I find that through times of solitude, I experience a deeper personal communion with the Lord. I am reminded that, although God loves all of us, God also loves me, specifically me, me as an individual. That is, God loves Jim Thomas. And while I don't understand *why* God loves me, when I get alone with Him, I am stirred at the wonder of it all, and He leads me to rest in the still waters of His unconditional love.

In the purity of silence, marked only by the rhythm of my heartbeat and the traffic of air through my lungs, once I have finally stopped talking, once I have turned off the myriad of voices clamoring for my attention in this world, I can get down on my knees and begin to rest at the feet of the Good Shepherd.

I found an old song lyric that expresses it well:

> *The LORD is my shepherd,*
> *I shall not want.*
> *He makes me lie down in green pastures;*
> *He leads me beside quiet waters.*
> *He restores my soul;*
> *He guides me in the paths of righteousness*
> *For His name's sake.*
>
> *Even though I walk through the valley of the shadow of death,*
> *I fear no evil, for You are with me;*
> *Your rod and Your staff, they comfort me.*
> *You prepare a table before me in the presence of my enemies;*
> *You have anointed my head with oil;*
> *My cup overflows.*
> *Surely goodness and lovingkindness will follow me*
> *   all the days of my life,*
> *And I will dwell in the house of the LORD forever.*
>
> Psalm 23

Rest, little lambs. Rest in Him.

- What does it mean to trust God?

- How can we be sure God has our best interest in mind?

- Is God trustworthy?

- How can trusting God help me with my fears?

5

Trusting:
How can I learn to trust God more?

> In God, we live every commonplace as well as the most exalted moment of our being. To trust in Him when no need is pressing, when things seem going right of themselves, may be harder than when things seem going wrong.
>
> *George MacDonald*

I LIKE TO DRIVE. No, let me rephrase that. I like to be the one doing the driving.

There. I admitted it. I'm a control freak. Trusting others just doesn't come easy to me.

One of the reasons I was drawn to my wife is because she has what I call an SRF (strong right foot). By that I mean she doesn't hesitate to use the skinny pedal on the right when she's driving. She doesn't speed and she's not at all reckless, but she does drive with determination, and when navigating traffic calls for decisiveness, she can rise to the challenge.

However, in spite of my appreciation for Kim's driving acumen, I still have difficulty turning over the wheel to her.

When we're going somewhere and she's the one driving, I say dumb things like "You might want to turn on your lights, it's getting dark." For some reason I don't think she'll notice that the big fireball in the sky is going down, the moon is coming up, and the street lights are flickering on.

Then, after she pulls out of the driveway, there are other things I feel compelled to remind her about. Traffic patterns. Directions. Use of blinker. Following too close. Speed limits. Getting in the right lane to exit, and lots of other strategic driving moves I would make if I were the one behind the wheel.

Understandably, all of this is quite annoying to her, and eventually she makes me aware of it by offering to pull off the road and turn over the keys. She's not being snippy. She's right. I need to let go. I need to trust her with the driving. I need to be reminded of my obsession with control.

Trusting others doesn't come easy for me. Even when the person I should be trusting is trustworthy. Even when the task is small. For some reason, it's hard for me to trust someone else to be in charge.

Trusting God can also be very difficult for me. It's not that I doubt God's ability. I know that if God can create and manage the entire universe, He must be capable of handling the problems in my little life. I'm just not sure about His resolve to manage things *my* way.

Leaving the Driving to Him

At times God seems unpredictable, and I can't figure out precisely what He is up to, which way He is leading me, or why. I pray, and then pray some more, hoping to gain some clarity. But sometimes, even when my world seems to be falling apart, heaven appears to be running silent. Isn't God listening? Doesn't God care?

Has that ever happened to you? If so, don't worry, you're not alone. There are many of us. We may have varying levels of anxiety and different things we like to control, but the problem is still the same. We basically have difficulty trusting God because it means we have to let go of the steering wheel and leave the driving to Him.

How should we handle our hesitancy and inability to trust God? That question reminds me of a day in the life of Jesus' disciples that is recorded for us in the fourth chapter of Mark's Gospel.

> On that day, when evening came, He [Jesus] said to them [the disciples], "Let us go over to the other side." Leaving the crowd, they took Him along with them in the boat, just as He was; and other boats were with Him. And there arose a fierce gale of wind, and the waves were breaking over the boat so much that the boat was already filling up. Jesus Himself was in the stern, asleep on the cushion; and they woke Him and said to Him, "Teacher, do You not care that we are perishing?" And He got up and rebuked the wind and said to the sea, "Hush, be still." And the wind died down and it became perfectly calm. And He said to them, "Why are you afraid? Do you still have no faith?" They became very much afraid and said to one another, "Who then is this, that even the wind and the sea obey Him?" (verses 35-41).

It was none other than President Franklin Roosevelt who said "We have nothing to fear but fear itself," but I'm still not sure I can agree with him. I believe in the correspondence theory of truth, which says "Truth is that which corresponds to reality." Reality tells me that this world is a very dangerous place, and the fact is, you can get hurt out there! There are a thousand things that can happen to you. You can drown in a stormy sea, get bit by a snake, fall off a ladder, contract a rare Himalayan disease; there are any number of things that are worthy of your fear.

For you chronic worriers, if you ever run out of things to worry about, there's a book with a list of things you might not have thought of before. It's full of fears that are sure to catch your worrying eye. It's called *The Paranoid's Pocket Guide* (Chronicle Books, 1997) and includes examples like these:

- One in 6500 Americans will be injured by a toilet seat during his or her lifetime.

- If you sneeze too hard, you can fracture a rib. If you try to block a sneeze, you can rupture a blood vessel in your head or neck and die.

- Nearly a third of all bottled drinking water purchased in the United States is contaminated with bacteria.

- Each year you face a 1 in 13 chance of suffering an accident in your home serious enough to require medical attention.

- Seventeen people are electrocuted every year by hair dryers.

- Last year, nearly 16,000 cheerleaders required emergency-room treatment for injuries including sprains, torn knee ligaments, skull fractures, and even paralysis. One of the most dangerous routines, the Human Pyramid, has been banned in North Dakota and Minnesota schools.

I don't want you to become paranoid, but just think about the risk factor involved if you were a cheerleader who caught colds easily, drank bottled water, and used a hair dryer everyday!

The fact is, all of us have to face some pretty scary stuff in life. Trusting God is not just an option for us, it's a necessity! But as we look a little closer at the story of Jesus and the disciples out on the stormy sea, perhaps we'll see that trusting God is also a wonderful privilege, a privilege that can set us free from living a life filled with anxiety.

The Significance of Trusting in Christ

By recording the account of Jesus calming the storm, Mark wanted to remind us that when our life becomes difficult—as if we're out on a lake during a violent storm, our sails and oars useless, our boat filling up with water, our ship ready to go down—even in those stressful times, those of us who are followers of Jesus still have an option. What is that option? What can we learn from the boat trip Jesus took with His disciples? There are three main points I see in this story.

Trusting Christ Doesn't Mean We'll Always Have Smooth Sailing

Now, please don't get mad at me. I know what you're thinking and I've thought it too. When we first believed in God, He was in the same category as Santa Claus, the Easter Bunny, and the Tooth Fairy. God was one of those wonderful children's fairy-tale characters whose job it was to make sure we're always safe, comfortable, and happy. How could it be God's will for us to have to go through storms?

As we grow up, we come to realize how this kind of thinking is really a trivialization of the life of faith. It's a shallow, self-centered view of who God is and the "good" He wants to bring about in our lives. The reality is, our spirituality is worked out in the real world, where life throws at us both curve balls and the stress that accompanies them. Our spiritual life is simply not compartmentalized from the other parts of real life.

We live in a fallen world, and Christians are not exempt from going through storms. We don't get to sidestep all of the stuff that sometimes makes life incomprehensible and almost unbearable. All the same bad things happen to those who place their trust in Christ that happen to everyone who does not trust Christ. Anyone who tries to tell you different isn't telling you the truth. When the storm that Mark describes came up, it took the disciples completely by surprise. It was overwhelming, sudden, and shocking. They knew their lives were in danger, and they were filled with fear and anxiety.

If we use the disciples' storm as a metaphor, what could a storm represent in our lives? Storms could be pictures of those unforeseeable and unavoidable events in our lives that startle us, stun us, and knock us off balance. Just like physical storms, these events can be large and overwhelming or small and annoying. They can be like destructive hurricanes, or like showers that drop just enough rain to get your car dirty.

Storms might symbolize the divorce of a couple you always thought would make it, or something as small as stubbing your toe on the bathroom door. They might represent an automobile accident, or a minor argument at a family gathering. They might signify hearing your dentist say those two words we all dread—"root canal"—or having a business luncheon fall through. The metaphor touches more on the unexpected nature of these events, the way they can catch you off guard and throw you for a loop.

Why Me?

When most of us encounter a storm, the first thing we do is ask questions such as, Why is this happening to me? Did I forget to pray today? Is God mad at me? Was I unkind to children or small animals yesterday? Although these may be honest questions and may possibly be helpful at times, they really do miss the point. Storms aren't always a result of sin or our lack of spiritual discipline. God is not in a spiritual slap fight with us, and the storms we encounter in life are not always some kind of punishment for the wrong things we do or the right things we fail to do. Just look at the way it happened in the lives of the disciples that day.

Whose idea was it to get into the boat in the first place? Who said, "Let us go over to the other side"? That's right, it was

Jesus' idea. What were the disciples doing when the storm hit? They were in the boat taking Jesus to the other side. They were in the right place, doing the right thing, at the right time. They understood what Jesus wanted them to be doing and where Jesus wanted them to go, and they were following His lead. But the will of God is not *always* about doing. It is, however, *always* about becoming, about learning, and about growing in our trust of God.

In the Scriptures we see that storms represent a couple of different ways that God acts in our lives. Sometimes there are *storms of correction* and sometimes there are *storms of perfection*. In the case of the prophet Jonah—a man who rebelled against God, refused to go where God told him to go, boarded a ship headed in the opposite direction, got caught in a storm, was thrown overboard, and was swallowed by a large fish—his storm was a storm of correction. God used the storm to correct Jonah in the same way a loving parent would correct an errant child. With the disciples, Jesus was using a storm of perfection to develop their trust in Him and cause it to mature.

Seeing Our Need for Jesus

Jesus decided He wanted to get away from the crowds and go over to the other side of the lake. Some of the disciples owned boats and were probably thinking, "We're professional fishermen, we make our living out here on the water, we know this lake like the back of our hands. We can handle this." They might have even said to their master, "Jesus, you sit here in the back of the boat, take a nap, and we'll get you over to the other side of the lake safely. Don't worry about a thing, we've got it all under control."

And it was then that the carpenter took the *fishermen* for a little boat ride. As I said, trusting Christ doesn't always mean it will be smooth sailing, and isn't it true that God sometimes takes us into the territory we're most familiar with, the one we think we have the most control over, and then stirs it up, shaking it from top to bottom so that we'll learn just how foolish it is to think we are in control?

It's during those times of stormy weather that we are humbled from our arrogance and come to recognize how much we really need the Lord in our lives. That appears to have been the lasting impression this event had on the lives of Jesus' disciples. As they recounted this experience years later in the New Testament books, I find it interesting that they didn't dress it up with a bunch of yardarm spin to make themselves look better. They could have told it more like this: "You should have seen us! The wind was blowing, the boat was filling up, we were all paddling as hard as we could. Things were looking grim, but then our master, Jesus, woke up, and He threw in with us. It was an awesome night that we'll never forget! We survived the perfect storm of '28!"

No, Matthew, Mark, and Luke are all pretty honest about the fact that on that day the disciples completely panicked. This was no legendary seafaring tale. The disciples were humble enough to tell us about their real fear during this real storm.

Jesus was tired, having had a couple demanding days healing lepers, casting out demons, preaching, and teaching. In spite of the miracles He as the Son of God performed, Jesus was also human. He got tired, and so He fell asleep while the disciples began to move the boats across the lake.

All of a sudden, a violent storm rose up. Mark says "there arose a fierce gale of wind, and the waves were breaking over the boat so much that the boat was already filling up" (4:37). In Matthew's account of this event, we are told "there arose a great storm *on the sea*" (8:24). The Greek word used here for "storm" is *sisemos*. It can be used to refer to a tempest, such as a gale force wind above the sea, or to a violent shaking within the sea. If the word refers here to an earthquake underneath the lake, a tremor like this would have caused a phenomenon similar to holding a large bowl of water in your hands while trying to run with it, the bowl shaking, the water rocking from side to side and spilling all over the place.

Evidently, the waves became so massive that they were breaking over the top of the boat. At the same time there was also a storm in the sky above the waves. The wind was blowing at gale force, and it was nighttime, so it was pitch black out. I can imagine the disciples had to be shocked and caught off guard. As their boat was filling with water, their hearts were filling with fear. This was it, they were going to die. Their ship was going down. They could see their lives flashing before their eyes.

Mark tells us there were other boats along that night. I can imagine the people in those boats thinking back to the miracles they'd seen Jesus do earlier that day. They were probably bemoaning the fact that Jesus hadn't sailed with them! And this brings up the second thing this passage teaches us.

Trusting Christ Does Mean We Always Have Someone to Turn To

What's the best thing to do when you're afraid? Get around someone who isn't. Here I have another confession to make. When I was just a little boy, there were times I was afraid of the dark. My mom would tuck me in, turn off the light in my room, and close the door, and on many nights, from the very first minute I would see all kinds of monsters and goblins in the shadows from the window. It didn't take long for me to jump up and go running down the hall to my mom's room so I could climb in bed and snuggle up next to her. She could protect me, she wasn't afraid, and being next to her calmed my fears.

The disciples finally figured this basic principle out too. They were afraid, and so they turned to Jesus. And what does Mark tell us Jesus was doing? That's right, He was asleep, the only guy that could help them was catching some z's. That's like when the plane is going down and the pilot is out cold!

Do you ever think, "My ship's going down and God's asleep at the wheel"? Do you ever wonder where God is when you are going through a storm like this? I have too. So did the disciples that day. In Mark 4:38 you can almost hear the disciples screaming: "TEACHER, DO YOU NOT CARE THAT WE ARE PERISHING?" And when the disciples finally turn to Him, Jesus is there for them.

I'm not a parent, but I'm impressed with those people who are. They can go to a party at a friend's house with their baby, set the baby on a bed in the guest room to sleep, go down and join the party with all of the music, laughing, and story-telling; but if their baby makes one little "waaaaa!" the parents can hear right through all the other noise and tell that it's their child's cry. I believe that in spite of the fury of the storm in your life, no matter how much confusion rages, when you cry "Lord, have mercy!" it never falls on deaf ears. He can hear your cries. He knows what you are going through. You can always turn to Him.

This storm didn't bother Jesus at all. He slept right through it. I'm convinced Jesus knew the storm was coming. As a matter of fact, He may even have arranged it and then used it to develop the disciples' faith in Him.

Notice the response of Jesus after the disciples finally came to Him. Jesus asked them "Why are you afraid? How is it that you have no faith?" (Mark 8:40). Ever the master teacher, Jesus was connecting the dots for the disciples. He wanted them to see that their lives depended ultimately not on their boat, not on their sailing skills, not on the weather, but on their trust in Him.

When Jesus rebuked the winds and the sea, they became perfectly calm. Mark says that Jesus told the storm "Hush, be still." The Greek word is *phimoo* and it means literally "Be muzzled." In effect, Jesus said to the storm, "Put a lid on it!" or "Zip it!" And Mark reports that "the wind died down and it became perfectly calm" (4:39). Upon Jesus' command, the earthquake (if that was part of the phenomenon) and the wind both subsided, and the sea became calm. With a storm that violent, in the natural order of things it would have taken hours for the sea to stop rocking back and forth and the waves to calm down.

In this memorable event, the disciples saw Jesus do something no ordinary person could do. He controlled nature. And this brings me to the third thing I see in this passage.

Trusting Christ Is Always Well-Placed Confidence

A child once prayed: "Dear Jesus, please help Mommy and Daddy. Take care of big sister and me. And please, God, take care of Yourself 'cause if anything ever happens to You...we're all in BIG trouble. Amen!"

Profound insight from such a young mind. Not that anything could ever "happen" to God, but profound in the recognition that we are all utterly dependent on God. The apostle Paul, speaking about this same Jesus, tells us that "by Him all things were created, both in the heavens and on earth, visible and invisible, whether thrones or dominions or rulers or authorities—all things have been created through Him and for Him. He is before all things, and in Him all things hold together" (Colossians 1:16-17).

In other words, Jesus is one with God, and Jesus created everything and even holds everything together by His mighty power. Reminding ourselves of this is one of the best ways to encourage ourselves to trust in the Lord. Studying God's Word and reflecting back on all the times when God showed Himself to be both capable and faithful to His people builds confidence in our hearts and gives rise to a tenacious trust in God.

The point I'd like to make from the story of the disciples on the stormy sea is that Jesus was contrasting fear of storms with trust in Him. As disciples ourselves, we may choose to listen to our fears and thereby silence our trust in Christ, or we may choose to trust in Christ and begin to silence our fears. Fear says "This storm is too big" and that we're destined to go down, as pawns of chance in a godless world. Trust says that even though there is a real storm raging, the real God who is there is really able to deliver us. He can bring us through the storm. We may get drenched, we may even drown, but ultimately we place our confidence in the One who created the sky and the sea and everything in this world. He is the One we trust with our lives.

Trust—A Habit of the Heart

Trust is not a one-time thing. It is not just a past event. We don't say, "I trusted God on May 20, 1976," as if that were the end of it all. You may have begun to trust God on May 20, 1976, but now you must learn to trust Him as a way of life—daily, moment by moment. It must become a habit of heart and mind for all of us. We must learn to trust Him in the calm weather so that when we encounter the stormy weather, we are not caught off guard.

This is precisely what the disciples were beginning to see. Mark tells us that after the storm subsided, the disciples became even *more* afraid. Sounds as though they were taking a step backward, doesn't it? But there is a fear that leads us to be afraid, and there is another that leads us to awe, respect, and wonder. One is an unhealthy fear, the other a healthy one. The disciples were afraid (unhealthy fear) of the storm, but they now feared (healthy fear) Jesus.

This person in their boat had just performed a miracle in which He had controlled the vaster forces of nature. They'd seen bodies healed, lepers cleansed, blind eyes opened, but up to this point, they hadn't seen anything like this, and it utterly blew their minds. Who was this Jesus, that even the wind and the sea obeyed Him? This is clearly what Jesus wanted them to think about. Through unique events like this, Jesus continued to establish in their minds exactly who He was: the very Son of God, the One who loved them, cared for them and had come to rescue them. More than anything else, Jesus wanted them to learn they could trust Him.

The disciples began this story fearing the storm and ended it fearing the Lord, which teaches us a great life principle: *When you have a healthy fear of God, you don't need to have an unhealthy fear of anything else.*

Throughout the Scriptures, one of the most often repeated commands given by God or an angel who represents God is "Do not fear." God, speaking through the prophet Isaiah, reminds us,

> *Do not fear, for I am with you;*
> *Do not anxiously look about you, for I am your God.*
> *I will strengthen you,*
> *Surely I will help you, surely I will uphold you with My*
> *   righteous right hand.*
>
> 41:10

And again,

> *Do not fear, for I have redeemed you;*
> *I have called you by name you are Mine!*
> *When you pass through the waters, I will be with you;*
> *and through the rivers, they will not overflow you.*
>
> 43:1-2

At the same time, the Scriptures are replete with commands for us to fear the Lord. Is this a contradiction? Not at all. Because of our sinfulness, we are inherently afraid of God. We are anxious and afraid of what will happen when God judges us, afraid that He will one day find us out. That's why Adam and Eve ran and hid from God after they first sinned. They were ashamed, and they were afraid of God. But the God of the Bible is not interested in a bunch of cowering, frightened children who run away from Him in fear for their lives. On the contrary, Jesus was showing the disciples on the stormy sea that He was eager to have them come running to Him. Run to Him when you are in a storm. Run to Him when you have sinned. Run to Him when you are confused. He is eager to have you trust Him.

When Fear Leads to Trust

There is a sense in which the things we fear are actually the things we trust. When the disciples thought their ship was going down, the reason they were afraid is because they thought if they lost their ship, then *all* was lost. Their trust was in their ship. But Jesus wanted them to place their trust in Him. We must learn to place our trust and confidence in the Lord, not in the things that are in this world. Ultimately, our jobs cannot save us, our relationships cannot save us, our health, wealth, popularity, and power cannot save us. God alone can save us. God alone is worthy of our ferocious trust.

Trusting God is not just about trusting Him to save us for eternity. It's also about trusting Him in the present moment, in today's weather, whether it be stormy or calm. Fearing the Lord is a handsome habit of heart, and the benefits of fearing the Lord are numerous we are told. "The fear of the LORD is the beginning of knowledge." "The fear of the LORD prolongs life." "The fear of the LORD leads to life, so that one may sleep satisfied, untouched by evil" (Proverbs 1:7; 10:2). Finally, in Proverbs 14:26-27 we are told, "In the fear of the LORD there is strong confidence, and his children will have refuge. The fear of the LORD is a fountain of life, that one may avoid the snares of death."

What tremendous promises, promises that can fuel our trust of God! This is not simply blind optimism. Optimism is based on temperament and mood; trust results in hope, and as believers, our hope is based not on the mood of the moment but in placing our trust and confidence in the infinite, personal God and what He has said in His Word. God knows about the storms in your life, and He can use them to develop your trust in Him. Trusting Christ doesn't always mean smooth sailing, but trusting Christ does mean we always have Someone to turn to, and trusting Christ is always well-placed confidence.

Trust Leads to Peace

Isn't it true that when you live through a storm like these disciples did, you lean harder into God? Don't experiences like this draw you closer to the Lord? How many times have you seen the Lord take what was a negative and transform it into a positive?

A wise man once said, "There are many things in life that will catch your eye, but only a few will catch your heart... pursue those." That's what happened to these disciples of Jesus. He caught their hearts that day on the stormy sea, and all but one of them trusted Him for the rest of their lives.

Christian spirituality does not offer a simple solution to a complicated problem; it's not just "Don't Worry, Be Happy!" It is "Don't worry, trust God, He is in control, He will take care of you." The peace that God gives to Christ's disciples is not the absence of trouble, but rather the confidence that when you walk through a storm, He will walk with you, and whenever you need to, you can turn to Him. His calming presence will always be with you.

Thomas à Kempis said:

> To preserve peace in time of trouble our will must remain firm in God and be ever directed towards Him, that is, we should be disposed to receive all things from the hand of God, from His justice, and from His bounty, with humble submission to His blessed will. Good and evil, health and sickness, prosperity and adversity, consolation and dryness, temptation and tranquility, interior sweetness, trials and chastisements, all should be received by the soul with humility, patience, and resignation, as coming to us by the appointment of God. This is the only means of finding peace in the midst of great troubles and adversity.

Remain firm in God. Direct your heart and mind toward Him. Find your peace in the fact that He is trustworthy and is always in control.

There was a story in the devotional magazine *Our Daily Bread* a few years ago that told of a group of scientists and botanists who were exploring remote regions of the Alps in search of new species of flowers. One day they noticed through their binoculars a flower of such rarity and beauty that its value to science was incalculable. Unfortunately, it was down in a tight ravine with steep cliffs on both sides. To get the flower, someone very small would have to be lowered down the cliff on a rope.

A curious young boy was watching nearby, and the scientists told him they would pay him well if he would agree to be lowered over the cliff to retrieve the flower below.

The boy took a long look down into the ravine and said, "I'll be back in a minute." A short time later he returned, followed by a gray-haired man. Approaching the botanists, the boy said, "I'll go down there and get that flower for you if this man holds the rope. He's my dad."

King David said, "When I am afraid, I will put my trust in You" (Psalm 56:3). When you trust someone, it isn't because you control the outcome. Trust is not always accompanied by knowledge. Sometimes I have no idea what God is up to in my life. Sometimes, I simply have to trust that getting into His presence is the answer.

Trust grows in a relationship over time. The longer I walk with the Lord, the more I am convinced He is trustworthy. God is the One I can turn to, the One I can trust to hold the rope or get me through the storm.

- How can we learn more about spirituality and spiritual growth?

- Can the Bible help in this area?

- How should we interpret the Bible?

- Are we supposed to take everything in the Bible literally?

- How should we apply the message of the Bible in our lives?

6

Learning:

How do I interpret and apply the message of the Bible?

> The [written] Word is the wire along which the voice of God will certainly come to you if the heart is hushed and the attention fixed.
>
> *F.B. Meyer,* The Secret of Guidance

NOT LONG AGO, I RECEIVED A FORWARDED e-mail from a friend who knows how much I enjoy dealing with questions. The content of the message (whose original source is unknown) was a list of simple, sometimes humorous questions that cause you to think about how often we miss the rather obvious. Here are a few examples:

- Why isn't phonetic spelled the way it sounds?

- Why are there interstate highways in Hawaii?

- If a cow laughed, would milk come out her nose?

- If you're in a vehicle going the speed of light, what happens when you turn on the headlights?

- You know how most packages say "Open Here"? What is the protocol if the package says "Open Somewhere Else"?

- Why do we drive on parkways and park on driveways?

- Why is it that when you transport something by car, it's called a shipment, but when you transport something by ship, it's called cargo?

Some things in life are obvious, some things become obvious after you give them just a little thought. When it comes to spirituality, if there's one thing that's become more and more obvious to me, it's that spiritual growth doesn't happen automatically. You don't just lie back as if to say "Okay, God. I've accepted Christ as my Savior. Now, You do Your thing. Hit me with holiness!" and then ZAP!—all of a sudden, you're a more godly person, you have a more effective prayer life, and you run around always singing songs from the latest praise and worship CD.

In the context of Christian spirituality, we come into a relationship with God by grace alone through faith alone. This means that all the hard work has been done by God, we simply respond to the free gift God has offered us by placing our trust in Christ. Our salvation cannot be achieved, it must simply be received. But this is just the starting point of the Christian life. Then we begin the process of following Christ and nurturing spiritual growth in our everyday lives, and it is this part that requires more active participation from us.

Nurturing Spiritual Growth

Spiritual growth is fostered in the same way my wife goes about working in the garden in our backyard. Every spring, she begins to weed, seed, and feed, and then stands back and watches as God brings about the growth. It might appear on the surface that Kim is doing most of the work, but when you think about what it takes to create and manage a universe containing just the right kind of solar system, with just the right kind of planet, with just the right kind of complex ecosystems, to provide an environment suitable for plant life, not to speak of human life…well, you probably get the point. Both God and Kim are involved in the overall goal of growing a healthy garden in our backyard. God provides all the power, Kim helps to nurture the growth. This is similar to the way it is for us as we pursue the goal of growing spiritually.

Spiritual growth (what theologians call *sanctification*) requires a partnership between God and us, a kind of *concurrence*. In no way does this idea negate our total dependence on God's grace. We don't "score points" with God because we are involved in our spiritual growth. God already loves us beyond measure. But if we are to grow, it does require effort on our part. As Dallas Willard has said, "Grace is not opposed to effort, it is opposed to earning." Our job is to weed, seed, and feed, but it is God who causes the growth. Concurrence reflects what the apostle Paul meant when he urged believers to "work out your salvation with fear and trembling," realizing that it is "God who is at work in you, both to will and to work for His good pleasure" (Philippians 2:12-13).

How do we weed, seed, and feed ourselves spiritually? What do these metaphors represent in practical terms?

Just as weeding a garden involves removing undesirable things that are growing in it, spiritual weeding might be confessing our sins and turning away from undesirable words, thoughts, or deeds in our lives. This requires repentance and experiencing God's forgiveness (which I have focused on in chapter 9 of this book).

Seeding a garden means planting those seeds we want to grow into healthy plants. In our spiritual lives this might be sowing the seeds of God's Word in our hearts and minds, that is, learning through reading, meditating on, and coming to a fuller understanding of what God has said through the Bible.

Feeding a garden includes watering and fertilizing. Spiritually, this might be nurturing our growth through the spiritual disciplines of worship, prayer, fasting, solitude, giving, and service.

In this chapter, I want to focus on seeding: learning from God's Word. Learning leads to growth. The apostle Paul told us that "faith comes by hearing, and hearing by the word of God" (Romans 10:17 NKJV). The Bible makes it clear that God really does want us to know Him and also to know something about Him. As we study the Scriptures, God's Spirit speaks to our minds and hearts, leading us deeper into our relationship with Him. Spiritual learning results in deeper knowledge, belief, and understanding. It involves the mind, the will, and the heart.

Faith Seeking Understanding

If you're like many people, you've probably had an experience where you opened the Bible at random, read a few verses in some book like Leviticus, and then determined you didn't have a clue what in the world the Bible was all about. Especially since you don't own a one-year-old she-goat, and even if you did, you aren't too sure you'd have the stomach to sacrifice it on the church altar as a burnt offering.

The fact is, for most people the Bible can sometimes be hard to understand. Interpreting what the Bible actually says and applying it to contemporary life can also be difficult. When trying to interpret what the Bible says, we are looking for its *meaning*. When trying to apply what the Bible says to our lives, we are looking for its *significance*.

In *Coffeehouse Theology* I discussed the reasons why you can be confident the Bible is God's Word. Here, I'd like to discuss some ways you can find both meaning and significance in what God has communicated through the Bible.

I was following a car the other day that had a bumper sticker on it that read: "Give Me Ambiguity or Give Me Something Else." It reminded me of how some people prefer spirituality to remain separated from reason and logic, limiting their spiritual life to only the mystical, experiential, and undefinable. But why should we compartmentalize spirituality off into the irrational and subjective side of life, leaving our minds completely out of the picture? God gave us minds. Doesn't He expect us to use them?

Anselm of Canterbury, who lived from about 1033–1109, thought so. He defined theology as "faith seeking understanding," and this begins to clarify what's so exciting about Christian spirituality. It calls for a full integration of faith into all of the rest of life and suggests that you don't have to leave your mind behind when it comes to spirituality.

When a lawyer of the Pharisees approached Jesus and asked Him, " 'Teacher, which is the greatest commandment in the Law?' Jesus replied: 'Love the Lord your God with all your heart and with all your soul and with all your *mind*.' This is the first and greatest commandment" (Matthew 22:36-38). Jesus was quoting from the Hebrew *Shema* found in Deuteronomy 6:5, but interestingly, the Shema only mentions loving the Lord with all your heart, your soul, and your *might*. For the lawyer of the Pharisees, a person who made his living with his mind, Jesus changed "might" to "mind." (Since the Scriptures are God's Word, the Son of God had a right to do that.)

When you step back and look at the complete picture, you see that the combined message of the Old and New Testaments is that we are to love God with all that we are, with all that we have, with all that we do, in essence, with every faculty of our being.

Loving God with our mind happens when we spend time reading the Bible, meditating on its timeless truths, and prayerfully considering how God might want us to apply those truths to our life.

Approaching the Bible

I can't tell you how many times I've opened the Bible and begun to read without giving the least bit of thought to what I was doing. It's like that old joke about playing Bible roulette: A guy is desperate for guidance from God, so he cries out, "Lord, speak to me!" He throws open his Bible and randomly reads the first verse his eyes fall on, which says "And he went out and hanged himself."

Not satisfied with that, the fellow closes the Bible, riffles through the pages again, reiterates his prayer "Lord, please speak to me!" and opens the Bible back up—and reads "Go thou and do likewise."

Obviously, this isn't a great way to approach reading the Bible, especially if you are looking for its true meaning and significance. God gave us brains and expects us to use them, including when we are reading His Word. So how should we approach reading the Bible?

The apostle John recorded something Jesus said that has helped me with my approach toward reading the Bible. In John 16:13, Jesus tells us that the Holy Spirit will guide us into all the truth. Here's that idea of concurrence again. Once I've taken the time to read the Word and humbly pray, asking the Holy Spirit to guide me into the truth, Jesus has promised that the Spirit will lead me to something that will help me grow spiritually. Sometimes it's truth for my mind, sometimes it's encouragement for my soul. Other times it's a warning about some temptation I may be struggling with.

The point is, we need to approach the reading of God's Word alert and with anticipation. So before you even open your Bible, ask yourself this: Are you approaching it expecting to hear from God? As F.B. Meyer has said: "The [written] Word is the wire along which the voice of God will certainly come to you if the heart is hushed and the attention fixed."[1]

This is the kind of thing Jesus was referring to when He would say, "He who has ears to hear, let him hear." We all have two sets of ears, those on the sides of our head and those in our heart. If the ears of your heart are inclined toward God when you approach the Bible, you are in a much better condition to hear the voice of the Holy Spirit as He leads you into a greater understanding of God and His truth.

Another important element in our approach to reading God's Word is having a teachable disposition. The question to ask ourselves is this: Do we truly desire to know what God thinks about a specific subject? Even if it runs against what we'd prefer to hear? Or are we simply looking for God to agree with the position we hold? One of my favorite Bible teachers, John Stott, expressed it this way:

> If we come to Scripture with our minds made up, expecting to hear from it only an echo of our own thoughts and never the thunderclap of God's, then indeed he will not speak to us and we shall only be confirmed in our own prejudices. We must allow the Word of God to confront us, to disturb our security, to undermine our complacency and to overthrow our patterns of thought and behavior.[2]

Interpreting the Bible

Once we have our hearts turned toward heaven in our approach to reading the Bible, how do we go about interpreting what we read in the pages of Scripture? Do you have to have a seminary degree to understand it? People will say, "Well, that's your interpretation. Everyone is entitled to their own interpretation." But does their attitude justify reading almost anything you want into what the Bible says? Should we completely disregard the idea that each of the original authors had something specific in mind as he wrote?

The Clarity of God's Word

The Westminster Confession makes it plain that the Bible is clear enough in all its central teachings for anyone to understand.[3] That doesn't mean there aren't some difficult passages, it just means the most important ideas are conveyed in a clear, easy-to-understand way. It also doesn't mean we won't benefit from listening to trained Bible teachers and theologians. It just means the basics of what God wants us to know are accessible to anyone who approaches the Bible with a hungry heart and an open mind. The only requirement is that we have to open the book and actually read what it says.

The apostle Paul, who wrote two-thirds of the New Testament, summed it up this way as he was writing to his young protégé Timothy:

> Continue in what you have learned and have become convinced of, because you know those from whom you learned it, and how from infancy you have known the holy Scriptures, which are able to make you wise for salvation through faith in Christ Jesus. All Scripture is God-breathed and is useful for teaching, rebuking, correcting and training in righteousness, so that the man of God may be thoroughly equipped for every good work (2 Timothy 3:14-17 NIV).

Notice again these phrases: "from infancy you have known," "able to make you wise for salvation," "useful for teaching, rebuking, correcting and training in righteousness," "so that the man of God may be thoroughly equipped for every good work." Paul wouldn't say that about a book whose meaning was either unclear or completely up for grabs. On the contrary, Paul's view of Scripture was that it had been clear to Timothy when he was much younger, and now that he was a young adult, the Scriptures would be clear enough to help him with spiritual and moral clarity and correction.

The Power of God's Word

Long before the apostle Paul wrote those words, God spoke through the Old Testament prophet Isaiah and declared, "So is my word that goes out from my mouth: It will not return to me empty, but will accomplish what I desire and achieve the purpose for which I sent it" (Isaiah 55:11 NIV).

Did you catch that? God intends for His word to accomplish something and to achieve something. Some of the literary images of the Bible clarify what God intends His Word to accomplish and achieve. In the vivid poetry of Psalm 119, the psalmist says, "Your word is a lamp to my feet and a light to my path" (verse 105). How might we interpret what this is saying? The metaphors "lamp" and "light" clearly refer to something that will illuminate what would otherwise be dark. The metaphor "my feet" could refer to where I am standing right now, my immediate life situation. "My path" could refer to the future just ahead or around the corner.

Sometimes the path we walk in life can be dark and uncertain, but into that darkness comes the light of God's Word to brighten where we stand now and to cast light in the direction we should turn next. The Word of God helps us evaluate the present, to see if what we are currently doing is in His will. It helps us discern the wisdom of God for our future steps in life, enabling us to make wise choices that will preserve our integrity and bring glory and honor to Him.

Handling the Scriptures Accurately

There are many good ideas about how to get the most out of a passage. Above all, we must keep in mind that we are dealing with the Word of God, which was written down in space-time history, but has eternal significance. Therefore, interpreting and applying the Bible is really more like an art than a science. As Paul wrote to Timothy, "Be diligent to present yourself approved to God as a workman who does not need to be ashamed, *accurately handling* the word of truth" (2 Timothy 2:15). How can we make sure we are handling the Bible accurately?

The answer to that question can get a bit involved, and it might seem to read like the directions for assembling a riding lawn mower. But if you've got a large cup of coffee going and can hang in there with me for a few paragraphs, I'd like to give you some tips I've found helpful in my own study of God's Word.

1. *Read through the entire passage casually.* Try to get the overall gist of what is being said. Take note of who the key players are, what action takes place, and especially how God, Jesus, or the Holy Spirit are involved.

2. *Identify the literary genre of the passage.* This is critical for accurately interpreting the passage. The Bible is rich in literary styles and before you can accurately interpret what a passage is saying, you should identify what kind of literature you are reading. You shouldn't interpret or apply the poetry of the Psalms the same way you would the direct statements found in the Ten Commandments. Some of the literary genres found in the Bible are:

- *Historical narrative*—Some have suggested as much as three-quarters of the Scriptures is historical narrative. This genre gives us the historical account of the relationship between God and humankind and can be found throughout the Old Testament books such as Genesis, Exodus, and Judges. In the New Testament, books such as Luke and Acts are rich in historical narrative. This kind of literature describes actual historical events, such as when God made His covenant promise to Abraham, when God delivered the people of Israel out of bondage in Egypt, the struggle of Israel with its neighbor nations, the life and times of Jesus, and the birth and growth of the early Christian church.

- *Law*—The Bible is full of God's instruction for moral and ethical behavior. There is *apodictic* law, which refers to the general principles of God's law, such as those expressed in the Ten Commandments. (Webster defines *apodictic* as "expressing...necessary truth.") These laws were delivered directly by God to the people, written out on stone tablets.

Then throughout the New Testament, Jesus and the apostles dealt with the application of the law to those they were speaking or writing to.

In the Old Testament there are also individual *case* laws, which clarified what the people of Israel were to do in very specific situations. In addition, there are *civil* laws and *ceremonial* laws, which gave them guidance in societal and religious matters.

Most Bible scholars agree that while the apodictic law remains relevant to contemporary situations, individual Old Testament case laws, civil laws, and ceremonial laws are no longer pertinent.

• *Prophecy*—There appear to be two kinds of prophecy in Scripture, *fore*telling and *forth*telling. A prophet was doing the former when predicting what would happen in the future, and the latter when speaking on behalf of God, pointing out sin or calling the people to some specific action. Interpreting prophecy can be difficult because it is often highly symbolic and metaphorical, and some prophecies have more than one fulfillment.

• *Poetry*—The book of Psalms is a good example of biblical poetry. It is filled with beautiful lyrics and poetic images. Hebrew poetry bears little resemblance to much of modern poetry, which can sometimes end up being simply about coming up with words that rhyme. The Psalms are deep, honest, and direct, expressing a wide range of human experiences and emotions.

• *Wisdom Literature*—The book of Proverbs is a good example of wisdom literature. It is full of short, pithy sayings that might contrast a wise person with a foolish person or give practical instruction for life. Wisdom literature can be found throughout the Old Testament Scriptures, especially in Ecclesiastes and Job.

- *Epistles*—Epistle means "letter." In the New Testament certain books were actually letters written to a specific group of people dealing with a specific teaching error or moral problem. Epistles include books such as Galatians, Ephesians, and Philippians. Interpreting these books must always be done with an awareness of what was going on with those people, in those locations, at those times.

- *Parable, metaphor, hyperbole, and so on*—In His parables, Jesus used earthly stories to make heavenly points. He made up many stories in which common, everyday things like coins, sheep, weddings, and farming became metaphors, similes, and analogies to teach His listeners about the kingdom of heaven. Most parables have one main point with an occasional secondary point or two. We should avoid overinterpreting the parables by trying to assign significance to every little detail.

  Jesus also used hyperbole, that is, exaggerating for effect, as when He said, "If your right eye makes you stumble, tear it out and throw it from you." It would be a grave mistake to make a literal interpretation of this command. Jesus knows we would struggle just as much with lust having only one eye. In the context of this passage, He's pointing out that temptation not only comes from without, but also from within. Nowadays, we aren't as used to hearing hyperbole as Jesus' contemporaries were, and reading a passage like this can cause some of us a great deal of anxiety (and possibly some pain!) as we try to figure out what it really means.

- *Apocalyptic literature*—There are books of the Bible that include highly symbolic imagery representing the struggle between God and the forces of evil. They include the book of Revelation and portions of the books of Daniel, Isaiah, Ezekiel, and Zechariah. Interpreting these passages can be difficult, and there are differing views on how to do this. But the good news is that, even if you have little idea how to interpret the details of apocalyptic passages, you can rest assured that, in the end, God always wins.

Identifying the literary genre of the passage you are studying will be immensely helpful as you seek to discover what God is saying through that passage. There are other ways of classifying biblical literature, and if you desire to look into this further, I highly recommend the book *Let the Reader Understand* by Dan McCartney and Charles Clayton (Wheaton, IL: Victor Books, 1994).

3. *Learn as much as you can about the author's historical-cultural setting.* This can be critical to finding out what the author intended to say. We have a quite different understanding of so many things today, from social habits to spiritual disciplines to civic duties. What was it like when the writer was alive? What was his political, social, or cultural setting like? What language did he speak? Who was he addressing when he wrote?

There are some great Bible study reference tools that can help you with historical-cultural research. You might pick up a study Bible like the NIV *Study Bible* or the *New Geneva Study Bible.* And there are a great many resources that can help you with more intensive study.[4]

(If you're still with me, you deserve to stretch, yawn, and take another sip of your favorite java!)

4. *Set the scene of the passage.* By this I mean visualizing in more detail the "who, what, when, where, and how" of the passage. Take special note of the key people and places involved. How many people were there? What were the surrounding buildings and terrain like? What action took place? What conflict or tension arose? Sometimes the richest learning comes from imagining yourself walking around the dusty walls of Jericho in the fourth row back with the Israelite marching band. Or going out on the boat with the disciples on the stormy sea. Or singing praise choruses while chained to a wall in a dark, damp, rat-infested prison cell with Paul. The purpose of setting the scene is not to read something into the text that isn't there, but rather to support the main point of the text by bringing some details to life.

5. *Allow what is clear to interpret what is not so clear.* If you're having difficulty figuring out what is meant in a certain passage, look for something about that same subject from another passage of Scripture. This is often called the "analogy of Scripture" or "allowing Scripture to interpret Scripture." It's a very important tool in staying true to the message God is trying to convey to us through His Word. For example, if you were wondering why Jesus keeps referring to Himself as the "Son of Man," you could cross-reference Daniel 7:13, where you'd find out that was a title that signified the Messiah who was to come.

6. *Distinguish between the descriptive and prescriptive passages.* The historical book of Acts is largely *descriptive.* It describes events, for instance, what happened when the Holy Spirit came at Pentecost to permanently live in every believer for the first time. There was an upper room, a mighty rushing wind, and "tongues as of fire," and the apostles "began to speak with other tongues." Does this mean we must be in an upper room, should expect to hear rushing wind, see tongues of fire, and begin speaking with other tongues (other languages) when we become believers and are filled with the Spirit for the first time?

Clearly this passage is not meant to be *prescriptive,* that is, establishing teaching about how the Spirit will fill every believer. It is simply descriptive of what the Holy Spirit did on one particular and unique day. On the other hand, the book of 1 Corinthians contains mostly prescriptive material, including some direct teaching about the Holy Spirit and spiritual gifts from Paul the apostle. Prescriptive passages are much more appropriate for establishing biblical doctrine than descriptive ones.

Applying the Message of the Bible to Everyday Life

If we are going to learn and grow spiritually, we must begin to see that reading the Scriptures is not just about knowing information. It is also about *transformation*. For that to happen we must apply the truth of the Scriptures to our everyday lives.

This is a very sensitive thing to do, and it requires the guidance of the Holy Spirit. Without His leading, we can get into all kinds of strange thinking by mishandling of the truths of the Bible. So as you begin to wonder how a given passage might apply to your own life, pray and ask the Holy Spirit to lead and guide you. Remember that the Bible as a whole is about how much God desires to be in relationship with His people and how He has gone out of His way to make this possible through what Christ did on the cross. This concept should serve as a backdrop to virtually every passage.

One of the best things we can do when looking for appropriate applications is to ask ourselves what points of identification we might have with the original writer, the subject matter, or the original recipient(s) of the writings. Was the author struggling with something we are also struggling with? Does the subject matter talk about something directly relevant to our time? Were the original recipients of the passage distracted or discouraged in a way that we can identify with? These and other questions can help answer the "So what?" of the passage you are studying. They can lead you to practical application, as you find yourself identifying with Elijah's doubt, Peter's denial, or the Galatians' distraction from the message of God's grace.

The Bible and Spirituality

Christian spirituality has been compared to a journey. Once we make the initial commitment to follow Jesus, our spiritual journey has begun. Along the way, there are twists and turns, hills, thrills, and spills, blessings and blowouts. As with any journey, we must know which direction we're headed before we can make any progress.

If you live in Washington D.C., and you want to drive to Florida, which direction should you go? Could you head out in a northwesterly direction and ever make your way to Florida? I suppose you could, if you didn't mind going all the way around the globe before you ever made it to Florida. But most people wouldn't want to do that, and that's why we have things like maps. They tell us the best direction to head when we're traveling between two points. Florida is south of Washington D.C., and that is the best direction to head if you want to go there.

When we're looking for ways to grow spiritually, the Bible is the map that offers us the best information. It tells us which direction to go, what kind of terrain we must traverse, what kind of roads and highways we can expect, and some helpful information about the landmarks we'll see along the way.

The Bible has been carefully prepared by God for the spiritual pilgrim who takes the time to read and reflect on what it says. The Bible documents the interaction between God and humankind over the centuries. It shows us that we were all made with the capacity to know God and that we will find fulfillment in our spirituality only when we are in a right relationship with God. It warns us that, as we travel on our journey, along the way we will be tempted toward distrust, distraction, and despair. It equips us with knowledge about how we can resist those temptations and what to do should we fall down or wander off the main road.

The Bible deserves to be read, interpreted, and applied with respect for its Divine authority, with hope for its transforming power, and with an openness to discerning its benefits. And whatever we do with it, let's not think that merely reading and accurately interpreting the Scripture is all there is to learning.

Christian spirituality is not just about filling our minds with correct spiritual data. We were not created as machines, and we were not designed to have a "virtual" spirituality. Christian spirituality is about living in a dynamic relationship with God, and studying the Bible is learning from the Word that comes from God's heart. "For the word of God is living and active and sharper than any two-edged sword, and piercing as far as the division of soul and spirit, of both joints and marrow, and able to judge the thoughts and intentions of the heart" (Hebrews 4:12).

- *What is prayer?*

- *Does prayer work?*

- *Does God answer all of our prayers?*

- *Is there a right way and a wrong way to pray?*

- *Why does heaven seem so silent at times?*

- *What are the elements of effective prayer?*

- *What can we expect from God after we have prayed?*

7

Praying:
How can I pray more effectively?

Why is it that when we talk to God we are
said to be praying but when God talks to us
we are said to be schizophrenic?

Lily Tomlin

THE STORY HAS BEEN TOLD OF A YOUNG CHILD who sat on the
back pew of the church while her mom and dad joined the rest
of the congregation up front for a prayer meeting. The little
girl had her coloring book and sat quietly, listening to the lofty
prayers of the adults as she filled in pictures of barnyard animals. She didn't always color inside the lines, but she loved to
color.

The adults had been enjoying a prolonged time of prayer as
several parishioners spoke to God in turn. There were prayers
of thanksgiving for His bountiful blessings, praise for answers
to previous petitions, and lofty words of worship for the transcendent, Almighty God. The little girl couldn't understand
much of what they were saying since their vocabulary was too
far over her head, but she knew they were talking to God.

At one point between prayers, there was a moment of silence that lasted a few seconds. Hearing her opportunity, the little girl stood up on the pew and pronounced loudly: "Dear God: A, B, C, D, E, F, G, H, I, J, K,…" and went on through the entire alphabet. When she got to "X, Y, Z," she ended with a hearty "Amen!" and sat back down.

The startled congregation, broken from their reverent attitude, couldn't believe what had happened, and they turned and watched as the mother ran back to quiet her daughter.

"What are you doing, honey? We're trying to pray up here."

Her daughter answered, "I know, I know, I was too. I just don't know how to talk to God with all those big words, so I thought I'd just give the letters to God and let Him put them together the way He wants to."

The little girl didn't always color inside the lines, but she loved to color. She didn't know how to pray "formally," but she loved to pray. She knew prayer in a simpler way, more as the first ones to pray did, the ancients mentioned in Genesis 4:26: "Then men began to call upon the name of the LORD." The little girl's prayer wasn't formal, it was just an honest calling on the name of the Lord. In her young faith she instinctively knew what the Lord had said through the prophet Jeremiah: "Call to me and I will answer you, and I will tell you great and mighty things, which you do not know" (Jeremiah 33:3). She gave God the letters and waited for God to put together the words she needed as He saw fit.

Prayer is one of the central activities of Christian spirituality, because prayer is how we each personally connect with God. Whether it be out loud, in silent thought, quietly in our mind and heart, or meditating and listening for the subtle voice of God's Spirit, we have been given prayer as the most intimate means available for us to commune one on one with God.

My prayer life is not always as honest as that little girl's, and it's likely I have a shorter attention span than most young children. I'm one of those people who have trouble praying for very long in one sitting. (There are probably angels who high-five each other whenever I make it to the 15-minute mark!)

I also wrestle with not being able to listen very well in my prayer life, and that's because I'm usually doing all the talking. It's not that I'm a fountain of praise or adoration. I'm usually talking about me. And almost as soon as I tell the Lord about something I need His help with, my mind goes to work suggesting exactly how He should go about helping me. As if the God of the universe needs my advice on how to help me! It would be very difficult for me to just pray the alphabet and allow God to put the words together the way He wants to. That little girl can teach me a lot about prayer.

Have you ever known someone who prays out loud really well? Someone who can turn a simple blessing at the dinner table into an awe-inspiring moment? Not because of their frequent use of "thees and thous" from King James vocabulary, not because they use words like "transcendent" or "omniscient," but because there is something authentic in their simple and honest way of approaching God. When you hear them pray, you get the sense they are really talking to Him, that they've entered the throne room and are standing right there in the presence of the Almighty God. As their words rise, they begin expressing things you've been feeling or thinking but had no idea you were even feeling or thinking them. What is it about those kinds of prayers that rings so true and strikes such a resounding "amen" in our hearts? What is it about those honest and intimate prayers that makes us hunger to know God like they do? What is it about their words that urges us to plunge in and ask the tough questions about prayer, such as "Does prayer really work?"

Does Prayer Work?

Sometimes I have to ask a question before I can answer one. In response to the question "Does prayer work?" I think it's important to ask first what is meant by the word "work." If it means we always get what we pray for, the answer is obviously no. That doesn't happen for me or anyone else I know. It didn't happen for the apostle Paul or for Jesus. Just before Christ was arrested, He prayed three times that if it were possible, the cup of death might pass Him by. Thankfully, Jesus was committed to God the Father's answer.

The reason we don't always get what we pray for is because praying to God is not the same as rubbing a genie's magic lamp. Prayer is not wishful thinking or merely thinking positive thoughts. Prayer is calling on the name of the Lord, sometimes in praise, sometimes to make a request, and in both of these senses, prayer does indeed work. God always receives our praise; something wonderful happens to us when we lift up our hearts and voices in worship of the majesty, power, and wisdom of the living God. We always benefit when we get our focus off ourselves and fix our attention on the Lord. And God always welcomes our petitions and requests for wisdom, guidance, and help in time of need. But we must keep in mind that "petitionary" prayer means prayer that makes a request. Requests may be granted or may be denied. And the prayers that benefit us most acknowledge that God is far more wise than we, far more informed as to what will work for His greatest glory and our ultimate good.

Francis Schaeffer said,

> God is not a machine. I must not see Him as a vending machine into which I put a quarter and get out a candy bar in a purely mechanical fashion. He is personal, and thus in answering prayer He operates on the basis of what He knows is the best and wisest answer to that prayer, and not just in a mechanical reflex.

The point is, we can trust God. He has promised to supply all of our needs according to His riches in glory, and when we pray according to His will, He consistently backs up that claim.

Jesus on Prayer

One day while Jesus was spending some time in prayer, it seems that some of His disciples came near and stood quietly by, watching and listening. When Jesus finished praying, Luke reports that one of the disciples approached Him and said, "Lord, teach us to pray" (11:1).

Jesus' prayer time had obviously piqued the disciples' interest. I wonder what they noticed as they observed Jesus praying. Was there something special about His body posture? Did Jesus kneel down, close His eyes, bow His head, fold His hands? What about the terminology Jesus employed while He was praying? Was it wrapped in a display of confidence, what modern TV evangelists call "holy boldness"? Did Jesus pray to remind God of His duty to live up to His word?

Somehow, I don't think so.

Immediately following their request, Jesus taught the disciples some things about prayer. He used just 68 words to answer them, and many of us probably know what He said by heart. From the outset, it's clear that Jesus wanted to keep us tethered to certain truths about God and ourselves. The Lord's Prayer highlights these foundational truths and shows us what effective prayer looks like. And who better to get us on the right track about how to talk with God the Father than God the Son?

Matthew (6:9-13) records Jesus saying: "Pray, then, in this way:

> *'Our Father who art in heaven,*
> *Hallowed be Thy name.*
> *Thy kingdom come.*
> *Thy will be done,*
> *On earth as it is in heaven.*
> *Give us this day our daily bread.*
> *And forgive us our debts,*
> *As we also have forgiven our debtors.*
> *And do not lead us into temptation,*

But deliver us from evil.
For Thine is the kingdom,
And the power and the glory, forever.
Amen.'"

The Lord's Prayer offers us an example of what prayer should be and what it should be used for. What do we learn here? Taking a step back and looking at it as a whole, you'll notice that the first half of the Lord's Prayer has to do with God's glory, and the last half, with our good. The first three thoughts recognize and honor God, and the last three make requests of God.

Is there a right way and a wrong way to pray? According to Jesus, the correct way to pray begins first with giving God the proper recognition and place of authority He should have in our lives. The reason this is important is simply because God deserves it. Even if God had never answered a single prayer of ours, He is still God and therefore is worthy of our worship.

Second, the beautiful thing about beginning our prayers by recognizing God's greatness is that in doing so, we remind ourselves that we aren't praying to a powerless and distant deity, a lifeless religious symbol hanging over the altar, or an impersonal force in the sky. We are praying to the living God who is really there.

Praise for God's Glory

Jesus began this model prayer by teaching us how to address God:

"Our Father who art in heaven"

The first word of the Lord's Prayer, "our," is plural. As a matter of fact, the singular—"I," "me," or "mine"—never appears anywhere in this model prayer. Jesus says when you pray, say "give *us* this day *our* daily bread," and "Forgive *us our* debts, as *we* also have forgiven *our* debtors," and again, "Do not lead *us* into temptation, but deliver *us* from evil."

What's the point here? The Christian worldview includes the idea that, once you become a follower of Christ, you are not alone in the universe. Rather, as Christians we are inextricably a part of something much larger than ourselves. We are connected "horizontally" with all believers everywhere because God's Spirit unites us together in Christ. In Nashville, it means Watershed Bible Study is connected to Grace Community Church, to Christ Community Church, to St. Bartholomew's Episcopal, and to Belmont Church. And we are all connected down I-40 West to First Presbyterian Church in Memphis, First Baptist Church of Little Rock, Christ the King Church in Dallas, First United Methodist Church in Houston, Calvary Chapel in Costa Mesa, California, and every other church that names the name of Christ throughout the entire world.

While we may have some differences in minor beliefs, nonetheless, as followers of Jesus we are one in the common bond of Christ. As spiritual siblings, when we pray, we are all praying to *our* Father in heaven.

Not only are we connected horizontally to all believers but we are also connected "vertically" to God. In this first line of the Lord's Prayer we see three things about the God to whom we pray. The first thing is that God is *personal*. He is our "Father," not our "fog," "our fate," or our "force." A force cannot forgive. Fate cannot provide comfort. And fog cannot speak a word of truth. Only a God with a face, God our Father, can do all of these things.

The second thing we notice here is that God is *loving*. Jesus taught the disciples to pray using the word *abba*, an Aramaic word that can be translated "father," "daddy," or "papa." The God of the universe draws close to those who want to humbly draw close to Him in prayer with sincere hearts. To those, God is near and dear as a loving Father.

Perhaps your own thoughts of God have mostly been thoughts of fear. There certainly is a sense in which we should have a healthy fear of God, and I think we have lost sight of this in many churches. Yes, the God of the Lord's Prayer is awesome enough that we should fear Him, but He is also loving enough that we can trust Him and place ourselves under His tender mercy. As a loving Father, God wants His children to come to Him, to throw all our cares on Him, and to look to Him for guidance.

The third thing we see in the first line of the Lord's Prayer is that God is *supernatural*. We pray to our Father who is *in heaven*. Heaven is a word that appears 71 times in the book of Matthew, and it reminds us that God is not limited by the physical universe. As Creator of all, He is above all. Psalm 103:19 says, "The LORD has established His throne in the heavens, and His sovereignty rules over all." Psalm 19:1 tells us that "the heavens are telling of the glory of God; and their expanse is declaring the work of His hands."

In many of today's spiritualities, you are taught to pray to God "as you understand Him to be." That's the same thing as believing that we can create God in our imagination. I can't see how a God I create can be big enough to worship, to obey, or to serve.

How big is the God you pray to? Jesus tells us that the Father God of the Bible is big enough to truly be *God*, and even His name is to be revered.

"Hallowed be Thy name"

The author of Ecclesiastes tells us, "Do not be hasty in word or impulsive in thought to bring up a matter in the presence of God. For God is in heaven and you are on the earth; therefore let your words be few" (5:2). There is something to be learned here about how we at times trivialize God.

"Hallowed" means separate, holy, consecrated, revered. The name of God is separate from all other names, and is to be revered because it represents not just what we call Him, but who He is. When you and I pray with this understanding, it serves to remind us how awesome God is. We are calling on His mighty name, and He has promised to come to our aid. Our confidence is not in working ourselves into an emotional frenzy. Our confidence is not in our theological accuracy. Rather, our confidence is in the power and authority of the name of the living God. And the wonderful thing about this is, when you are weak, when you are doubting, when your soul is exhausted from the fight, you can trust that the effectiveness of your prayers does not depend on how you feel, but rather on the unlimited power behind the name of the Lord.

Calling on God's name is no mere superstitious use of the name "God," as if we would use it to cast a spell or in reciting an incantation. Rather, since God is personal, we honor His name most when we place our trust in Him. "Those who know Your name will put their trust in You, for You, O LORD, have not forsaken those who seek You" (Psalm 9:10). "Some trust in chariots and some in horses, but we trust in the name of the LORD our God" (Psalm 20:7 NIV).

> **"Thy kingdom come.**
> **Thy will be done,**
> **On earth as it is in heaven."**

Here is where we begin to get inside of how prayer works. In any kingdom, the king is sovereign, and the will of the king is to be done. In our prayers, we are to pray that God's will may be manifested here on earth as it is in heaven. "Earth" includes more than one level of human experience. We should pray for God's will to be done on a national, international, and global level. But we should also pray for God's will to be done in our communities, in our homes, and most importantly, in our own hearts.

Those who pray for God's will to be done do so because they believe God has shown Himself to be both wise and loving. God is the best qualified to decide what should be done in every situation of our lives. Just as we go to an expert to build a house, to fix a leaky pipe, or to get tax advice, God is the expert on life and on building character in us, so we go to Him and lay our lives in His hands. This is the safe place for our souls: under the rule of God our King.

So here in the first half of the most famous of prayers we have statements about the name of God, the kingdom of God, and the will of God. Christian spirituality is driven by a desire to see God's name honored in our lives, God's kingdom advanced in our lives, and God's will achieved in our lives. This is clearly a great way to begin any prayer, as it puts our minds and hearts in the right perspective. When we pray with a selfish heart our motives center around building our name, our kingdom, and our will; getting glory for ourselves, establishing our own power center, and making everyone and everything serve our own desires.

William Barclay once wrote, "Prayer is not a way of making use of God; prayer is a way of offering ourselves to God in order that He should be able to make use of us." And Leonard Ravenhill said, "Prayer is not an argument with God to persuade him to move things our way, but an exercise by which we are enabled by his Spirit to move ourselves his way." I have to confess that my prayers are all too often reduced to me taking my wish list to God. I don't always spend half, especially the first half, of my prayer times in worship and praise. But when I do, there is something amazing that happens to my view of all the things I care so much about. Suddenly, I find I am able to let go of those things that have tied me up in anxiety. And God has become so large that my problems have become small.

From Praise to Petition

> **"Give us this day our daily bread.**
> **And forgive us our debts,**
> **As we also have forgiven our debtors.**
> **And do not lead us into temptation,**
> **But deliver us from evil."**

Steve Brown says he knew of a man who used to start his day with this prayer: "Lord, so far today I haven't been grumpy, selfish, greedy, envious, proud, or angry. I'm really pleased about that. But in a few minutes I'm going to get out of bed, and from then on I'll probably need a lot more help."

I don't know about you, but I need a lot of help to make it through most days. Grumpy and his pals come far too easily to me! Fortunately, God has shown Himself to be faithful to me even when I've been faithless toward Him.

A number of movies and fairy tales have offered the following scenario: If you were granted just three wishes, what would they be?

I wonder how you might answer that question. What three things would you wish for? It certainly makes you consider carefully what your greatest desires might be. Should you go for cash, a car, a career, or a condo?

In this model prayer, Jesus instructs us to ask God for what He considers to be three of our most important needs: daily bread, forgiveness for our sins, and deliverance from temptation, evil and sin. It's revealing that the things we often spend time praying for are not even on Jesus' short list. But God is always thinking about what will meet the deep needs of our heart. He knows we have needs that go far beyond our greeds.

William Barclay points out that these three petitions in the Lord's Prayer represent the human experience in the *present*, *past*, and *future*. They are requests concerning provision for the present, forgiveness for the past, and protection from temptation and evil in the future.[1]

In addition to this, the three personalities of the Trinity are alluded to. When we ask for bread for our earthly lives, it brings to mind God the Father, our great Provider. When we pray for forgiveness of our sins, it brings to mind God the Son, our Redeemer and Savior, Jesus. When we pray for help with future temptations, it brings to mind God the Spirit, who warns and challenges us to avoid temptation and then gives us the strength to resist.

So here in the last half of this short prayer we are encouraged to bring all of our needs to all of who God is: the entirety of our lives, past, present, and future, to the entirety of God, the Father, Son, and Holy Spirit.

Have you ever wished you knew someone you could do that with? Someone you could be totally transparent with, someone you didn't have to hide anything from? Jesus tells us that God wants you to come, just as you are, tired, broken, battered, or embarrassed. None of that matters. God loves you and has opened the door for you to come to Him. He will become the refuge you so desperately need. He is the Source that never runs dry, and He is waiting for you to simply turn in His direction.

Back to the Beginning

**"For Thine is the kingdom,
And the power, and the glory, forever"**

The Lord's Prayer ends where it began, with the focus on God. That is what prayer is really all about, getting our hearts, minds and wills in line with His. In Jon Courson's words,

> God does not need our worship, but we need to wor-
> ship. When I'm at the place where I'm saying "For
> Thine is the kingdom, and the power, and the glory,
> forever" with open heart and raised hands, suddenly,
> I'm outside myself, lifted above my cares and worries,
> my hobbies and toys.[2]

"Forever" is a mysterious word. Tell some people they might live forever, and they can only imagine it as eternal boredom. If you're addicted to an anesthetized life of incessant distraction, boredom is what you get. However, an eternity spent in the presence of an infinite God suggests the probability of endless new discoveries and adventure.

In his book *Orthodoxy*, G.K. Chesterton points out that in some Eastern traditions there is a symbol for eternity that is a snake coiled in a circle with its tail in its mouth. While some modern people have adopted this symbol to represent their spirituality, Chesterton imagined what an unsatisfactory meal this must be for the snake. Here is an finite creature that remains stuck, repeatedly cycling around, coming back again and again to the same old same. That sounds like boredom to me.

In contrast, the central image of the Christian faith is the cross. A cross is the joining of a vertical beam and a horizontal beam, and it signifies the God of heaven intersecting humanity on earth in the person and actions of Jesus Christ. There is a sense in which the cross represents the Christian idea of infinity, because the cross can extend its four arms out forever. This, however, is infinity at its best, and it gives us a reason to look forward to every new minute we are given to live.

"Amen"

In the 68 words of the Lord's Prayer, there is instruction from Jesus on how to address the God of the universe. You can use it as a model or as a memorized prayer, and you can medi- tate on it for hours. But the point is that when we pray as Jesus taught us to, our prayers become dynamic and effective. In this sense, prayer always "works."

Prayer is where we most intimately connect with God, and He with us. This will require quiet, focus, and patience. Sometimes it will seem that heaven is silent, that no answer is coming, but remember, at the end of the day it is God Himself who will be the answer to our deepest longings.

As C.S. Lewis said in *Till We have Faces*, "I know now, Lord, why you utter no answer. You are yourself the answer. Before your face questions die away. What other answer would suffice?" Yes, we live in a real world with real needs and desires. We long to know what God want us to do with our lives. The ultimate answer is that God has made us for intimate communion with Himself—and what a great honor it is to experience His presence in prayer.

Draw near. He is waiting.

- *What is temptation, and how are we tempted?*

- *Is the devil a real personality or just an explanation for evil in general?*

- *What does the devil want from us?*

- *Is there a connection between spirituality and morality?*

- *How can we resist temptation?*

8

Struggling:

How can I win my struggle with temptation?

And gradually, though no one remembers exactly how it happened, the unthinkable becomes tolerable. And then acceptable. And then legal. And then applaudable.

Joni Eareckson Tada

IT IS SUGGESTED THAT BETWEEN FIVE AND SIX MILLION years ago, in a vast desert region of what we now call the western United States, a tiny stream of water rolled down the Colorado plateau. Following gravity, the wind, and the terrain, it headed in a southwesterly direction and began a process that would leave an indelible mark.

Now called the Colorado River, that stream still runs that same course today. Where there was once a smooth plateau, the river has cut a massive canyon, 1 mile deep, 18 miles wide at some points, and 277 miles long. It's listed as one of the seven wonders of the natural world and is popularly known as the Grand Canyon.

Ages ago, on one particular day, the land said yes to that small stream of water. And it kept saying yes over and over again until, after many years, the water eroded the land and the result is a deep, yawning canyon.

Some people think that when a marriage falls apart, it happens because one day, one person did something stupid that suddenly ended years of trust and commitment. But the problems of life aren't quite as simple as that. Somewhere way back, on a particular day, one person did say yes to something he or she should have said no to, and it split the oneness of the couple. At first it was most likely a "yes" of the heart or mind and not of the voice. Then over time, there were more "yeses" where there should have been "nos," likely on both sides of the relationship, and what was once just a small split in their oneness grew into a deep canyon, until their lives were eventually so separate, so torn apart, that both hearts were left broken.

Whether it is divorce, lying, gluttony, or gossip, spiritual erosion happens in our lives when we say yes to something we should have said no to, or conversely, when we say no to something we should have said yes to. The difference between us and the Grand Canyon is that we have a choice in the matter. Our moral choices are not predetermined for us by the laws of gravity, physics, environment, or even genetics. We are rational creatures created with the ability to make real moral choices. When we choose what is right, our lives and the lives of those around us may be enhanced. When we make wrong moral choices, the results are often devastating, both for ourselves and for those we claim to love. By making bad moral choices we erode our conscience and character, destroy precious relationships, and set poor examples, which younger, more impressionable minds are likely to follow later.

The erosion of our own soul may seem negligible at first, but over time it will leave us feeling dead inside, not as if we don't exist, but as if there's a *non-feeling someone* where *we* used to be. C.S. Lewis once said that every time we make a wrong moral choice, it leaves a scar on our conscience. Multiple scars soon create a callus. Eventually, our conscience grows numb and can no longer perceive the difference between right and wrong. Ignoring your conscience is like cutting a canyon through your soul. Eventually, your inner life is left torn apart, dry, lifeless, and empty, just like the desert walls of a canyon.

Keystone-Cop Christians

For most of my life I felt like a spiritual Keystone Cop. I was in motion, but I was tripping and falling all over the place as I went along. I spent a lot of time picking myself up, dusting myself off, and looking around in embarrassment to see who had witnessed my clumsiness. Then I started back on my spiritual journey again, progressing just a short distance before I'd stumble or fall down again. Looking back over the years, it seems as though I should have been able to figure out what things would trip me up, but all the falling down and getting back up kept me too busy, too distracted to even notice.

Jesus told His disciples to "keep watching and praying that you may not enter into temptation; the spirit is willing, but the flesh is weak" (Matthew 26:41). And the apostle Paul wrote that "no temptation has overtaken you but such as is common to man" (1 Corinthians 10:13), which means that in this life we can expect temptations to come, and that being tempted will be a common experience for all of us.

There's a difference between dwelling on regret and learning from the past. As I look back over my years of spiritual naiveté, my years of not noticing what was tripping me up, I now desire to "watch and pray," to pay attention, to ask for God's help both to see temptation coming and then to have the courage to resist and stand strong, with my faith and confidence in the Lord.

All of this poses several questions that we must deal with: Where does temptation come from? Is there really a devil and demons who are bent on enticing us to sin? If so, what are their strategies? Where are we vulnerable and how should we handle temptation?

Temptation

From the outset I want to make it clear that being tempted is not a sin in and of itself. Jesus was tempted, the apostles were tempted, and every human being who has ever lived has been tempted. It is how we *respond* to the temptations that come our way that determines whether we allow them to grow into specific acts of sin. The apostle James tells us that "each one is tempted when he is carried away and enticed by his own lust. Then when lust has conceived, it gives birth to sin; and when sin is accomplished, it brings forth death. Do not be deceived, my beloved brethren" (James 1:14-16).

Here we see the progression. It begins with temptation and enticement, if these are nurtured they proceed into sin, and ultimately the end is death. We are quite alive when we are tempted and are therefore capable of either resisting temptation or giving it a home in our hearts and minds. If we choose the latter, we will be carried away by the temptation and end up sinning, which ultimately leads us to spiritual death. Along the way, there is a subtle erosion of conscience and a slow, almost unnoticeable, death of the soul.

The Sources of Temptation

While the *strategic* use of temptation belongs to the devil and his demons, from Scripture it's clear that there are at least three distinct sources of temptation. They are usually categorized as the world, the flesh, and the devil. Since these may sound like outdated religious terms, let me explain what they mean in more contemporary language.

The World

What the Bible refers to as "the world" means *the way the world thinks and acts apart from God*. The idea is that the world's way of thinking stands in contrast to God's way of thinking. The world's way of thinking argues for unbridled pleasure, moral autonomy, and self-centered living. God's way is a life centered on Him, which brings moral responsibility and self-control. But just how is the world involved in our temptation?

We are all social creatures, and as a result we all have an influence on each other. Every day, each person is influenced by the ideas of others about what is right and what is wrong, about what will fulfill us in this life, and about what makes our lives significant and meaningful. Believers don't live in a glass bubble isolated from other ideologies, and so the world's way of thinking can be a source of temptation for us.

One example is what I have come to call the Culture of Flippancy. The world's way of thinking tells us that to be funny is the highest of social achievements. The first person to the clever one-liner wins, regardless of who gets hurt, or what is made light of, in the process. Now I love to laugh, and I think that Christians have the best reasons in this world to be laughing. But flippancy is a distortion of good humor. It's often used by those who are trying to hide their pain and want to avoid opening up to others. It can be used like a shield to keep a person from having to risk being known or loved. Flippancy keeps a person from growing deep and is the world's way of thinking apart from God.

Another example of the world's way of thinking is when you are doing your level best to take part in the family vacation, then all of a sudden somebody fails to treat you with the kind of respect you think you deserve. The world's way of thinking says, "Assert yourself! Don't be a doormat!" and so you are drawn to react, to strike back, and then comes an opportunity for the whole trip to the beach to be washed right down the sink as you "stand up and demand your rights."

The interesting thing is that the Christian way of responding would not have you be a doormat either. Rather, you maintain

your dignity not by blowing up or overreacting, but by courageously waiting for the appropriate time to go and talk to the
person who has offended you—after you have dealt with all of
your own issues, after you have prayed and asked God to help
you, and once you have adopted an intentionally humble attitude.

What we do with those urges to be flippant or to strike
back in anger reveals how we are dealing with the temptation
that comes from the world and whether or not we have the
courage to think differently than the world does. The prophet
Isaiah reminds us of the stark difference between God's way
of thinking and the world's: "As the heavens are higher than
the earth, so are My ways higher than your ways, and My
thoughts than your thoughts" (55:9). And the apostle Paul
warned us in Romans 12:2, "Do not be conformed to this
world, but be transformed by the renewing of your mind."
(Some people call religion "brainwashing for the weak-
minded." I agree with the songwriter Barry McGuire, who
once said that most of our minds could probably use a little
scrub once in a while.)

The Flesh

The "flesh" as a source of temptation? Now there's an idea that
conjures up images of a curmudgeon God who hates all forms
of pleasure. Fortunately, that God is not the God of the Bible.
As it relates to temptation in the Scriptures, this term is not a
reference to literal human flesh or any particular body parts.
The flesh refers to our sinful and distorted desires. Since sin is a
distortion of God's original plan, individual sins are often an
instance of some natural, God-given desire run amuck or
twisted into something *like* the original plan. But our nature is
sinful when we are born, and we are powerless on our own to
resist sinning. But when we become Christians and the Holy
Spirit changes us and begins to dwell within us, He gives us
both the will and the strength to be able to resist the sinful
urges of our flesh.

The Bible does not teach that our physical body is evil in and of itself. Christianity is not some kind of archaic prudishness that demands that its followers abstain from enjoying all forms of human pleasure. It was God who created food, sex, rest, and all other physical pleasures, and God is also the One who designed our bodies with the ability to enjoy them. The problem comes when we deviate from God's original plan for the way these things should be enjoyed. It is then that we have fallen prey to the flesh.

The Devil (and His Demons)

Thirdly, the devil himself or one of his underlings can also be a source of temptation. The Bible takes the existence of such beings for granted, and while it doesn't tell us precisely how these evil spirits tempt us, it does seem to suggest that they will take advantage of any opportunity to do so and may exploit the other two primary sources of temptation: worldly and fleshly thinking.

That's why on any given day you might find yourself looking up and to the left at just the right time and on just the right part of the road as you drive to work so that you will see a billboard with the enticing picture of a beautiful girl "selling" cars. The devil then takes the opportunity to remind you how you have become less attracted to your wife lately, and how your life might be a little more exciting if you could just go out with someone like that beautiful young model sprawled across the hood of that nice, shiny red car.

Or you might be standing at the magazine rack, looking over all of the latest hairstyles in fashion magazines and wondering why God had to make you with curly hair when straight hair is what is "in" right now. Stirring up desire and at the same time a dissatisfaction with existing aspects of our life is one of the main strategies of the devil.

His most direct efforts take place in our minds, where he seems to be able to speak in some way, to plant the seeds of thoughts and ideas. Since his most clever weapon is deceit, it is often through speaking in the first person that he will try to fool us. He will plant the suggestion "If I risk love, I might be rejected" or "Why did they get ahead and not me?" or "I can't believe she said that to me!" cleverly inflaming a thought at just the right time to bring about fear, covetousness, or conflict with others, which ultimately causes us to doubt God, become dissatisfied with ourselves, and fall into some sin. Once the devil succeeds at getting us to sin, he has the nerve, in one of his shrewdest strategies, to follow that right up by throwing thoughts of immobilizing guilt at us. He is called the "accuser" because he loves to tell us how guilty we are, even though he knows that God has forgiven us our sins.

That is why the apostle Peter warns us sternly: "Be of sober spirit, be on the alert. Your adversary, the devil, prowls around like a roaring lion, seeking someone to devour" (1 Peter 5:8). That's a powerful, graphic image, but one that Peter wants us to take seriously. What could he have meant by this? The devil is presented as our adversary, which means he wishes to bring about our demise. That he is "seeking someone to devour" simply means he is out to eat your lunch!

The Place of the Devil in Our Worldview

On Friday night, July 19, 1940 Adolph Hitler stepped up to the microphone and went on the radio to preach his ideology of lies to the thousands of people who would listen in that night. Little did Hitler know that on this particular evening, the noted Oxford University don and Christian apologist C.S. Lewis would be among those in his radio audience.

The next day, Lewis began writing a letter to his brother Warren to tell him about what he had heard:

> I don't know if I'm weaker than other people, but it is a positive revelation to me how while the speech lasts, it is impossible not to waver just a little. I should be useless as a schoolmaster or a policeman. Statements which I

> know to be untrue all but convince me, at any rate for
> the moment, if only the man says them unflinchingly.

Lewis was impressed with how the charismatic Nazi leader could make so many people believe his lies as if they were truth. That Sunday, Lewis went to church for a communion service and later that afternoon finished the letter to his brother:

> Before the service was over—one could wish these things came more seasonably—I was struck by an idea for a book which I think might be both useful and entertaining. It would be called 'As one Devil to Another' and would consist of letters from an elderly retired devil to a young devil who has just started work on his first 'patient.' The idea would be to give all the psychology of temptation from the other point of view.[1]

It seems that the persuasive skills of Adolph Hitler inspired Lewis to help us look behind enemy lines; to see humanity from the perspective of the father of lies; to see how the schemes and wiles of the devil are employed in the temptation of mankind. Lewis wrote the book, and it became one of his most popular works, *The Screwtape Letters*.

Red Tights, a Pitchfork, and a Cape?

Decades later, in our more technologically advanced era, belief in the devil and demons may, for some, seem suitable only in video games, TV, and movies, but not in the "real world" in which we live. What more can we find out about the devil, demons, and temptation? Can a biblical worldview offer help and practical advice for avoiding the moral, mental, spiritual, and emotional pitfalls that surround us and which have led to the demise of so many who claim to follow Christ?

Realizing that even among those who call themselves Christians there may be differences of opinion, I'd like to answer some of these questions by asking a few of my own, spinning off from what we've already seen in the Bible and from some of the ideas Lewis raised in *The Screwtape Letters*.

If for the sake of argument you grant that the devil does exist, and supposing you yourself were the devil, what kind of strategy would you use to make sure you could go about your business unfettered? Would you conduct your affairs in broad daylight or under the cover of darkness? Would you let us poor humans be aware of it when you were tempting us, or would you do things more covertly? And if we humans already believed in your existence, how would you like us to think of you? Would you prefer thoughts of that cute and clever little fellow in a red suit with horns, a pointy tail, and pitchfork? Or would you like us to think of you as the "dark side" of an impersonal spiritual force?

According to an October 1999 Barna Research Survey, some 59 percent of Americans believe that Satan is not a living being, but only a symbol of evil. If I were the devil, I'd be rather happy with that. I'd do all I could to keep people from taking me seriously or thinking about what I might possibly be up to when it came to their spiritual and moral condition.

More from the Bible About the Devil

You certainly don't need to believe in the devil to acknowledge that temptations exist. One can be tempted by an inanimate object as simple as a chocolate bar or by something as enticing as a sexual image on the Internet. No devil is needed for these things to draw us in, our appetite for such things is easily aroused.

Nonetheless, the Bible teaches that the tempter (another name it gives to the devil) is quite real. He is personal, and he is intelligent. Though we aren't told precisely when, sometime during the creation process God made the angels, and Lucifer (who became the devil) was one of the most beautiful of all the angels. God gave the angels moral freedom and in order to do that, just as with humankind, God also gave them the real option of rebelling against Him. Lucifer was apparently the leader of the angels who chose to rebel, that's why he and the angels who followed him are called "fallen" angels. Because of their rebellion, they were driven from God's presence and banished to this planet, where they await final judgment by God.

It's encouraging to remember that the devil is not on an equal footing with God. The devil is a created being and is the opposite of other high-ranking angels like Michael or Gabriel. The Bible clearly reveals that God Himself has no equal, that He is unique and is the only non-created entity. Knowing this can be of immense help to us as we seek to understand both the power and the limitations of the devil. Although a formidable foe, the devil is not all-powerful, not all-knowing, not all-seeing, and is not present everywhere. What power the devil does have is derived. It is not his own, and he is free to act only within limits laid down by God (see Job 1:12; 2:6).

That's the third source of temptation we are dealing with. Now let's take a look at temptation at work so we can learn more about how to deal with it.

Why Resistance Is Not Futile

Today in many cultural circles, indulging temptation is applauded as people worship at the altar of moral autonomy and unbridled passion. In his book *True Spirituality,* Francis Schaeffer expressed it this way: "we are surrounded by a world that says 'no' to nothing." Turning a blind eye to the personal costs of their indulgences, insensitive to the collateral damage and casualties caused by their lack of self-control, those who embrace such a cavalier and selfish attitude destroy families and ruin thousands of lives.

And since we are all born with the capacity, even predisposition to sin, sometimes it seems futile to resist. Temptation is a universal experience for us. But as Martin Luther pointed out, "I can't keep the birds from flying over my head, but I can prevent them from building a nest in my hair." Temptation is when the birds are flying over our head. Sin comes when we fail to put up the "No Vacancy" sign. Allow a temptation to build a nest, to take up residence in your mind—and before you know it, it begins to dominate your thoughts and leads you to a sinful action.

If the devil is such a formidable enemy, if worldly thinking and the flesh are such powerful forces, how can we win this struggle? How do we keep ourselves from becoming a walking wildlife reserve for every kind of flying fowl? Perhaps an example from the Scriptures will be helpful.

In Genesis 39 we find the account of a young Hebrew man named Joseph, who was sold into slavery, carried down to Egypt, and ended up as a servant in the household of Potiphar, the captain of Pharaoh's bodyguard. In spite of this negative set of circumstances, the Bible tells us at least five times that "the Lord was with" Joseph and blessed everything he did. As a result, Joseph was soon given responsibility over the entire household of Potiphar.

However, along the way, Potiphar's wife became attracted to Joseph and began trying to seduce him whenever Potiphar was away. From the very first time, Joseph told her "no," and he continued saying no, until on one occasion the woman grabbed Joseph's overgarment and would not let go of it. So Joseph literally stepped out of his cloak and ran away. The scorned woman held onto the cloak and showed it to the other servants and then to her husband, claiming that Joseph had tried to rape her. Potiphar seems to have had some doubts about his wife's story. He could easily have had Joseph killed for such an act, but instead, he threw Joseph in Pharaoh's jail.

Here is a case of intense sexual temptation. It's likely this woman was quite attractive, since she was married to a successful military man who probably had his pick of wives. Not only that, but she was aggressive, and Joseph had an opportunity to take advantage of her advances every time he was alone with her in the house. But Joseph answered ultimately to God, and he knew that God had declared that adultery was wrong. So he resisted the temptation, and even though he went to jail, he could have ended up dead.

Interestingly, we are told that the Lord was with Joseph even in jail, and later, he was released from jail, went to work directly for Pharaoh, and rose to the top position in Egypt just under Pharaoh himself. The repeated statement that the Lord was with Joseph tells us something about how we can resist temptation. It is the presence of the Lord in our lives that will release us from being prisoners to our sinful desires. The Holy Spirit is the One who will provide the power for us to resist those overwhelming urges that haunt us.

Learning to Resist

What can we learn from Joseph about how to resist temptation? It's really quite simple, though not necessarily easy. What did Joseph do the very first time Potiphar's wife approached him? He said "no." What did Joseph do every other time she approached him? He said "no." Then, when she became more aggressive and grabbed his clothes, what did he do? He ran for the hills.

Joseph's method of resisting temptation is a good one. Say no the first time. Say no the second time and every time after that. Then, if the temptation grows more intense, run for the hills and get as far away from the temptation as you can. That may sound like the coward's way out, but it's really not. It's simply a practical way of shooing the birds away. Joseph's strategy is "If they are going to build their nest *here*, then I am moving over *there*."

If you are wrestling with some temptation and having difficulty resisting, it may help to ask yourself a few questions such as these I found on the Internet:

- What settings are you in when you are tempted? Avoid them.

- What props do you have that encourage that sin? Eliminate them.

- What people are you usually with when you are tempted? Avoid them.

That's fairly practical advice, but I realize that at this point, someone may be saying, "That's simplistic. You don't know how hard it is for me, how difficult it would be to change things!" Oh yes, I do. Being a human, I'm well aware of the vise grip of sin. As my friend Randall Tex Cobb says, "Anyone who doesn't think sin is fun, isn't doing it right!" I'm aware that sin is fun, but it is also costly fun, and the long-term price greatly outweighs the short-term fun. What seemed like a warm Jacuzzi tub probably felt real good to the frog at the beginning, but then he boiled to death in the kettle. Sin is fun for a season. But then there are always consequences to be paid. And unfortunately, innocent people are often collateral damage along the painful path of the results of our sin.

No Unique Temptations

No matter what you or I may struggle with, the Bible tells us there is no such thing as a unique situation when it comes to temptation. In spite of how you might feel, you and I are not the first people on the planet to wrestle with the things that tempt us. Millions and millions of people before us have had the same basic struggles. At the end of the day, there are really just three responses to temptation: We can stand, we can flee, or we can fall.

Joseph used response number one for a while but eventually had to move to number two. Other men or women, including myself at times, go with response number one for a while but then cave in and skip over to number three. But the basic principle is this: You stand while you can, but you should flee before you fall. Running away is not for cowards. It takes moral courage to flee.

In 1 Corinthians 10:13, the apostle Paul tells us that "no temptation has overtaken you but such as is common to man; and God is faithful, who will not allow you to be tempted beyond what you are able, but with the temptation will provide the way of escape also, so that you will be able to endure it." So when you are out of strength to resist, what should you do? Start looking for God's way of escape. It may be the strength to stand. It may be the courage to flee. Perhaps it will be a refocusing of your affections or desires.

If you are struggling with temptation, keep in mind that Jesus came to restore and rescue those who want to be restored and rescued. He is the Good Shepherd who follows after the lambs who get distracted or deceived and then stray. Don't be afraid to be honest with God about your situation. Tell Him about it. Ask Him to deliver you from evil. Ask Him to lead you in the paths of righteousness. His mercies are new every morning, and that means each day can be a brand-new start for you if you trust Him.

These days, I don't worry so much about being a spiritual klutz because God regularly reminds me that this was the whole reason Jesus came to earth to begin with. God knows that all Christians are Keystone-Cop Christians. None of us is perfect, none of us has figured it all out, none of us walk a pure and consistent walk. But by His grace, we have been forgiven. What's important isn't how many times we fall down. What's really important to our spiritual progress in this life is how many times we get back up. And the good news is that it's not all up to us. We're not alone. He stands ready to lift us back up and set us on our feet, ready to dust us off, ready to put us back on the path of life again.

- Has God forgiven us for everything we have done, no matter how bad?

- Is all guilt bad?

- What can I do to free myself from this overwhelming sense of guilt?

- How can I experience God's forgiveness in my life?

9

Receiving:

How can I experience God's forgiveness?

Forgiveness is man's deepest need and highest achievement.

Horace Bushnell

MY MOM WORKS AT THE PENTAGON. I can't tell you much about the specifics of her job (for your own safety, of course), but let's just say she's involved in the military.

Early one evening, the phone in Mom's office rang when she happened to be there to pick it up. The voice on the other end was that of an older man who said he didn't know whether she was the right person to ask, but that he was interested in finding out whether the military had kept records of certain incidents that occurred during World War II. "Which certain incidents?" Mom asked. The gentleman cleared his throat, mumbled a little, and then told her what had happened.

He was a veteran and had been stationed in France during the war. One night he and several buddies left their base and headed for a bar in the nearby village. After several hours and far too much alcohol, they started back to the base. Along the way, they picked a fight with a man from the village and literally beat the poor fellow to a pulp. The victim hardly put up a fight. They left him by the side of the road, not even sure he was still breathing.

Later that night, back at the base, MPs came through their barracks, trying to find out who had done this. He and his friends stood in statue-like silence, afraid of getting found out. For more than 50 years, this man had lived with the burden of guilt for his unconscionable act.

The caller went on to tell my mom that recently he had become a Christian and after all those years, he felt that God wanted him to find the man and set things right. It's likely the man had had some expensive medical bills as a result of his injuries, and the caller wanted to make restitution.

My mom is the perfect person to have received this man's call. She's had a lot of experience saying things like "Don't you worry. God can take care of this. He loves you so much." God knows my mom's heart. She's seen both sides of forgiveness, and He directed this man's call straight to her desk.

Mom told the man that, unfortunately, there were no records like the ones he was looking for. During a war it's impossible to document everything, and in addition, some records are blown up, burned up, or otherwise destroyed during fighting. She then added that, by God's providence, his call had come to her, and that she too was a Christian. That being said, she encouraged him to acknowledge God's full forgiveness. He had done all he could. He had been sensitive to the conviction of the Holy Spirit. He had been willing to make things right, even though it might have cost him something. God had brought him to the place where his heart was soft again, the ears of his conscience healthy and hearing again. He was truly sorry and had honestly admitted his guilt. In becoming a Christian he had allowed God the joy of setting him free and wiping the slate clean, and now it was time to simply receive the assurance of God's forgiveness.

With a tearful stammer, the grateful old veteran thanked Mom and said goodbye, the burden lifted, the stain of his sin washed away. He had been humbled by experiencing the great forgiveness of God.

The Quiet Voice of Conscience

Someone has said, "Confession is good for the soul, but bad for the reputation." But what happens when the individuals of a culture become concerned about their reputation to the exclusion of their soul? Can any of us afford to prefer our reputation over our soul?

John Wooden, the former UCLA basketball coach, once said, "Be more concerned with your character than with your reputation, because your character is what you really are, while your reputation is merely what others think you are." We live in a culture that trivializes substance and worships celebrity. We are obsessed with image and appearances. Yet, it is the soul that is the seat of character and conscience. Conscience is the means God speaks through to call us to Himself, to convince us of what is true, to remind us of what is right and what is wrong.

Back during the war, the caller who spoke to my mom had learned to ignore his conscience. No longer stirred by its uneasiness, he was capable of great evil. Later, after he became a Christian, the Holy Spirit renewed the sensitivity of his conscience and then went on to lead the man to seek restoration. God sent him to my mom, one of God's agents of compassion, and she spoke the gracious words that confirmed God's forgiveness.

Wise King Solomon once said, "He who conceals his transgressions will not prosper, but he who confesses and forsakes them will find compassion" (Proverbs 28:13). That's so true. When our conscience is healthy, God uses it to flag us down, warning us of error and making us aware of our true guilt when we have done wrong. A healthy conscience is the relentless, haunting voice of God's Spirit in our lives. As Mark Twain quipped, "An uneasy conscience is a hair in the mouth." That's precisely what God designed it to be, the persistent, sometimes annoying reminder that we are headed down the wrong road.

Fortunately, in His mercy God doesn't leave us without hope. When we sin, we put distance between ourselves and the Lord. But God is in the business of restoration. When we confess and turn away from our sin, God restores us in His love and compassion. The road back may seem long, tedious, and sometimes costly, but as Max Lucado has said, "If there are a thousand steps between us and God, he will take all but one."

The Road to Restoration

You've probably heard the story of another person who was humbled by God's great forgiveness. In Luke 15 Jesus tells the parable of a prodigal son who was full of youthful pride and greed. He had an insatiable lust for autonomy. In his self-centered naiveté, he thought he didn't need his father, family, or anyone else. He demanded his share of the inheritance and left his family behind.

He headed off to a faraway land, with big plans to live it up and enjoy all that life had to offer him. But after a while, the young man ran out of money. As his fortune dissolved, so did his deluded confidence. Finally, he ended up working on a pig farm, feeding hogs, poverty-stricken. Desperately hungry, he wished he could steal some of the pigs' food.

Jesus tells us that one day the prodigal came to his senses. He recognized his foolishness and determined to head for home, planning to confess his sin and seek his father's mercy. He would try to convince his father to give him a job as a hired servant.

As he approached his family home, a surprising thing happened. From a distance, his father saw him coming. He ran out to meet his wayward son, thrilled to see him again, and he embraced him and kissed him.

Immediately the son began to confess his sinfulness, but the father said nothing. It was as if the father already knew how his son felt. Displaying an amazing grace, the father did not give one hint of "I told you so," rather, he put a ring on his son's finger, called for a fine robe to be brought, and ordered up some roast beef to throw a welcome-home party. In short, he fully restored his son with joy and gladness.

What a tremendous illustration of both the mercy and grace of God. The prodigal son didn't get what he did deserve (rejection), and he did get something he didn't deserve (restoration). Matthew Henry makes this insightful comment: "The prodigal came home between hope and fear, fear of being rejected and hope of being received; but his father was not only better to him than his fears, but better to him than his hopes." This is the way it is with our heavenly Father as well. We are all like the prodigal. We have all demanded our own way. We have all taken what the Father has freely given us and wasted it. We have all craved autonomy and unbridled pleasure and have left Him out of our lives.

But just like the prodigal, we have been offered a road to restoration with God. Once we recognize we have distanced ourselves from God, when we find ourselves out of our own resources, when we're lying face down in the mud of some far-away land, keenly aware of our bankruptcy and brokenness, then the Father reveals our road back home. Our way back to Him includes five simple elements.

Acknowledging Our Sin

First, like the prodigal, we need to *acknowledge our sin*. Like they say in the South, we need to "fess up," which means we must own up to the fact that we are in the wrong. Humans have perfected the art of blame-shifting. It started right after the very first sin was committed, when God asked Adam and Eve about what they had done. Adam's first words were "The woman you gave me...." Then God asked Eve the same question, and her first words were "The serpent...." Adam blamed Eve, Eve blamed the serpent, but nobody "fessed up."

Ever since the time of Adam and Eve, whenever possible, we have played dodgeball with our deserved blame and true guilt. We live in a false paradise of self-deluded innocence.[1] As Brennan Manning observed of the human race, "In a world where the only plea is 'Not guilty,' what possibility is there for an honest encounter with Jesus, who died for our sins? We can only *pretend* that we are sinners, and thus only *pretend* that we are forgiven."[2]

Now, as Christians, we must realize how counterproductive this is to receiving God's forgiveness. Forgiveness does not apply to faultless "mistakes" or things that happen "to us." Forgiveness is possible only when there has been an infraction, a breaking of some trust, a real offense. Sin is rebellion against God and the distortion of what He has called good. Sin is something we choose to do. It is willful disobedience. Masking it, renaming it, calling it a genetic quirk, an "unfortunate choice," an "illness," blaming it on our environment, our dysfunctional family, or anything else, does us no good whatsoever. We need to ask God to supply us with the moral courage to come clean and deal with our sin head on. Unless we acknowledge our real sin, we cannot experience real forgiveness.

If our conscience is healthy and is working as God designed it to, our sin will weigh us down. And in spite of what the preachers of pop psychology might say, I believe this is *good*, because our conscience is telling us the truth. God's answer for sin and guilt is not blame-shifting or denial, it is forgiveness. C.S. Lewis understood this when he said: "What we call asking God's forgiveness very often really consists in asking God to accept our excuses....What we have got to take to him is the inexcusable bit, the sin."[3] When we go before God, we must leave our excuses behind. We must "fess up" and acknowledge our sin.

Turning Away from Our Sin

Once we acknowledge our sin, the second element that moves us toward restoration can come into play, which is that we need to repent, or *turn away from our sin.*

What is repentance? The original Greek word is *metanoia,* and it means "a change of mind that institutes a change in life." Repentance means turning around. And when you are on the wrong road, that is exactly what you must do. If you are ever to make any real progress, you must turn around and go back to the right road, and begin heading in the right direction again. Turning away from sin means getting back to thinking as God does about what is right and wrong.

Repentance is not a mere exercise in thinking, it is not just academic or emotional assent to the fact we have sinned. Repentance is doing something about that which you say you believe. It implies that we have a choice and can take some action. It means we are not predetermined or preprogrammed to mess up by our environment, temptations, or genetics. There is dignity in repentance, in that it serves to remind us that our moral life is above fatalistic acquiescence. The apostle Paul confirms this: "no temptation has overtaken you but such as is common to man; and God is faithful, who will not allow you to be tempted beyond what you are able, but with the temptation will provide the way of escape also, so that you will be able to endure it" (1 Corinthians 10:13).

Confessing Our Sin

Next, we need to make a *genuine confession of our sin.* Have you ever had anyone apologize to you, and after they did, you still weren't sure they really meant it? Maybe they stated their apology like this: "I'm sorry *if* I offended you." That "if" sure can change the way an apology comes off. Perhaps we would all do better if we agreed that a genuine apology can never be stated with the word "if" in it.

A genuine confession involves admitting that real wrong was done. It means we clearly understand that we've offended the other person and caused him or her inconvenience, loss, or pain. But every sin we commit is also an offense against God. Though the action we took may have directly hurt our mother, father, brother, or sister, we have also offended our holy God by mistreating those people. Our sins are not just on the "horizontal plane," they are all "vertical" as well. When we sin, we need to go to God with a genuine confession and apology for our sins so that we can experience His forgiveness.

Some of us struggle with chronic temptation toward a specific sin and find ourselves confessing the same sin many times, over and over again. This may cause us to become hopeless or despairing over our repeated failures. Cornelius Plantinga compares confession of sin to a routine household chore: "Recalling and confessing our sin is like taking out the garbage: once is not enough." There are many people who wrestle with a certain sin and find themselves taking out the same garbage over and over again. But we shouldn't lose confidence in God's declaration that we are forgiven, since it is Jesus Himself "in whom we have redemption, the forgiveness of sins" (Colossians 1:14).

Forgiveness for Our Sin

If our journey down the road to restoration is to continue, we will need to realize that God has offered us *real forgiveness*. Humans are not good at this. We tend to bury the hatchet with the handle sticking out of the ground so we'll be able to find it and take it up again should the need arise. But God's forgiveness has buried both hatchet and handle. As Martin Luther King Jr. said: "Forgiveness is not an occasional act, it is a permanent attitude." Forgiveness is the permanent attitude of God and the standing promise of the Bible for all those who place their faith in Christ.

This is where Christian spirituality has infinitely more substance than the new spiritualities. Fate cannot forgive. An energy force cannot forgive. Only a God with a face, a personal God, can forgive. Before the God who will one day judge us all, the forgiveness of our sins was purchased by Christ once and for all when He died on the cross in our place. Jesus Christ paid the debt that we owed to God, and now, through Christ, we have real forgiveness, the only way to permanently deal with guilt and sin. And this brings me to the final step on the road to restoration.

Receiving God's Forgiveness

With grateful hearts and in true humility, we must *receive the forgiveness offered* by the grace of God. Here is how restoration becomes complete. On our end of things, God's forgiveness is not achieved, it is simply received. Its power is not dependent on the one who has been forgiven but on the One who did the forgiving. As my wife Kim has said in her book *Simplicity: Finding Peace by Uncluttering Your Life,*

> The truth is that our forgivability is not the issue. The issue is *who* the Forgiver is. At my very best, I am not deserving. William Langland said, "And all the wickedness in the world that man might work or think is no more to the mercy of God than a live coal in the sea."[4]

Our complete forgiveness was purchased by Christ's death on the cross. Once we have confessed our sin, we must refocus our attention from ourselves and our sin to Christ, remembering what He achieved for us through His death. The Bible teaches that "in Him we have redemption through His blood, the forgiveness of our trespasses, according to the riches of His grace" (Ephesians 1:7). We have been cleansed by the blood of Christ, which simply means that in the spiritual realm, before God, the slate has been wiped clean. And because of this, like the prodigal son's father, God welcomes us home with a full embrace, with joy and gladness!

Perhaps you are wrestling with something you have done that you know was wrong. Maybe you have a chronic problem with temptation and you think God has grown tired of forgiving you. We may try to lock our secret sins in a closet and throw away the key, hoping no one will find them out. But the problem is still on our own conscience. God knows about it too. Even the devil knows about it, and he will use that knowledge to accuse, immobilize, and demoralize us. Unless we unlock and open up the closet door, acknowledging our sin and brokenness, unless we admit we aren't perfect, and that we struggle with things like pride, arrogance, anger, bitterness, and lust, we will never be able to move down the road to restoration and freedom.

Let me encourage you to seize this opportunity to be set free from the guilt and pollution your sinfulness may be causing your soul. Acknowledge your sin, repent from it, and confess your sins to God. He won't be shocked by anything you have done. Over the course of human history, He has seen much worse, many times. God is not pleased that you and I sin, but He is thrilled when everything His Son achieved on the cross becomes effective in our lives.

Christian spirituality offers a unique answer to the problem of true guilt. It's a truly clear conscience brought about by real forgiveness through Christ. "If we confess our sins, He is faithful and righteous to forgive us our sins and to cleanse us from all unrighteousness" (1 John 1:9).

- *What does it mean to worship God?*

- *How can I connect with God in a more intimate way?*

- *How can being a part of a church really help me in my faith experience?*

- *What does it mean to come into the presence of God?*

10

Worshiping:
What does it really mean to worship God?

We must quit making God a practical deity who exists to help us succeed.

Calvin Miller, Into the Depths of God[1]

HER NAME WAS MARY TOO, BUT SHE DIDN'T do anything histor-ically significant like give birth to the Savior of the world. Her name was Mary too, but she didn't have a dramatic story to tell after having seven demons cast out of her. Her name was Mary too, but she was just Mary of Bethany, the sister of Martha and Lazarus. However, Mary of Bethany is mentioned four times in the New Testament, and there's a good reason why.

One time, Jesus had come to the home of Mary and Martha. Martha got busy preparing a meal while Mary sat at Jesus' feet listening to Him teach. Another time, when Jesus had shown up too late to heal Mary and Martha's brother Lazarus before he died, Mary ran to Jesus, fell at His feet, and began to express her confusion at why He had not arrived ear-lier. A third time, during the week before Jesus would face death on a Roman cross, as He and the disciples were sitting down for dinner, Mary came to Him with a bottle of extremely expensive cologne, broke the bottle open, poured it over His feet, and then wiped them with her hair. The fourth time, after Jesus' crucifixion and burial, Mary saw Him risen from the dead, and she ran to Him and clung to Him, falling at His feet to worship Him.

Where was Mary all four times we read about her? That's right, she was at the feet of Jesus. What was she doing? She was listening to His teaching, she was confessing her confusion and looking for His guidance, she was expressing extravagant devotion to Him, and in all these things, she was worshiping Him.

What Is Worship?

It's interesting that the Bible never really offers us a direct definition for worship. In the Scriptures, there are several different terms used in connection with the idea of worship. The most often used New Testament Greek word is *proskuneo*, which includes the idea of showing reverence to, honoring, or bowing to. It comes from the words *pros*, which means "toward," and *kuneo*, which means "kiss," and it has some connection with the ancient Greco-Roman practice of kissing the ground to honor the earth and its deities. You can probably imagine what this very physical expression of worship might look like. It looks a lot like Mary of Bethany.

Our English word "worship" comes from an old English word that means "worthship," which means to show respect or honor to someone or something because of its worthiness. When we turn to talking about the worship of God, there are broad and narrow definitions we might use. In a broad sense, all of life can be seen as worship. The way we behave, the thoughts we think, the things we say, everything about our lives can reflect the honor we desire to show to God. In a more narrow sense, worship refers to those special times when we pause from our other activities to express our devotion to God. It is this more narrow sense that I would like to focus on.

Worship is one of the most important aspects of Christian spirituality. When we worship, we pause to encounter God, we humbly bow and express our love for Him. We find ourselves focused on God, drowning in the delight of simply being in His presence. It's an experience of intimate communion with God in which we may be startled by His holiness or awestruck by His transcendence and His complete otherness. As we draw closer to God in worship, we may be silenced by His majesty and yet, somehow, emboldened by the assurance of His love toward us.

I'd like to focus on four foundational questions that will help us understand what worship really should be. These questions are relevant to private worship by an individual or public worship by an assembly of believers. They should be helpful to anyone honestly trying to learn how to come into the presence of God, commune with Him, and worship Him.

1. What Is the Purpose of Worship?

The Scriptures are packed with terms and phrases that give us some clues to the purpose of worship. Many of them represent specific expressions or acts of worship. We are told, *Bless the Lord! Magnify the Lord! Praise the Lord! Exalt His name! Seek the Lord, remember His wonderful deeds. Ascribe to the Lord the glory due His name!* These statements, among others, begin to give us an idea of the true purpose of worship.

When we worship God, we acknowledge who He is, declaring that He is uniquely worthy of our praise. We passionately proclaim His glorious power, His unmatched creativity, and His boundless generosity. And we express our heartfelt thanks and devotion to Him.

The word "glorify" may bring us closest to understanding the purpose of true worship. King David said, "I will give

thanks to You, O LORD my God, with all my heart, and will glorify Your name forever" and "Tell of His glory among the
nations, His wonderful deeds among all the peoples" and
"Ascribe to the LORD the glory due His name" (Psalm 86:12;
96:3; 1 Chronicles 16:29).

To glorify means "to boast." In a discussion about worshiping God, this may sound a little strange at first. We all
know people who boast about themselves, their accomplish-
ments, or their abilities. Sometimes what they say may be
nearly true, but most of the time when people are boasting, it
strikes us as self-indulgent, and often they are overstating the
facts to make themselves look better than they really do.

When we glorify the Lord, we are simply boasting about
Him, and there is virtually no chance we could ever overstate
the facts about His greatness. The infinite God is far more awesome, far more wise, far more powerful, far more loving and
patient than any of us could ever imagine. When declaring the
things about God that are worthy of praise, we don't need to
worry about going overboard.

> "Let not a wise man boast of his wisdom, and let not
> the mighty man boast of his might, let not a rich man
> boast of his riches; but let him who boasts boast of this,
> that he understands and knows Me, that I am the LORD
> who exercises lovingkindness, justice and righteous-
> ness on earth; for I delight in these things," declares the
> LORD (Jeremiah 9:23-24).

When the early Christian church first got together, worship
was a prominent part of their activities. Luke records that just
after Jesus ascended into heaven the disciples were continually
in the Temple, praising God (Luke 24:51-53). A few weeks later,
on the day of Pentecost, the disciples stood up and began to
speak of the "mighty deeds of God" (Acts 2:11), and the Lord
added thousands of people to the new church. Luke tells us
that "every day they continued to meet together in the temple

courts. They broke bread in their homes and ate together with glad and sincere hearts, praising God and enjoying the favor of all the people" (Acts 2:46-47 NIV). From the get-go, the church worshiped God, glorifying the Lord, boasting in Him, and speaking of His mighty deeds.

At the time of Jesus, being religious had replaced being in relationship with God, just as it has in some churches today. But just like Peter, James, John, and the rest of the early Christian church, we are not without hope. For all who hunger to return to the Lord in authentic worship, the Holy Spirit stands waiting to light the flame of renewed faith as we offer up a sacrifice of praise.

If we go back further in time, we can listen to King David as he reveals his idea of the purpose of worship in one of his songs:

> *I will bless the LORD at all times;*
> *His praise shall continually be in my mouth.*
> *My soul shall make its boast in the LORD;*
> *The humble shall hear it and rejoice.*
> *O magnify the LORD with me,*
> *And let us exalt His name together.*
>
> Psalm 34:1-3

For David, worship meant to bless the Lord, to praise Him out loud, to boast in Him so that all those who are humble of heart would hear it and be glad.

Understanding the purpose of worship can help clarify another aspect of worship, which leads us to the next question.

2. What Is the Focus of Worship?

A friend forwarded me a story about a visitor to an Australian ranch in the Outback, who asked the owner why he had so few fences. "How can you keep track of your cattle without fences?" the visitor asked. "Simple," replied the rancher. "Out here we dig wells instead of building fences. Cattle are highly motivated to stay within reach of their source of life."

God is the wellspring of life. He is the Source of truth, love, peace, and joy. When we really understand this, we are motivated to draw close to Him, to fall at His feet, to acknowledge our need of Him, and to worship Him.

Sometimes we can stray away from these things and find that our expression of worship is directed by what will merely entertain or amuse us. This a grave error in spiritual focus. The "audience" of worship is not ourselves or those who attend our churches. The audience of worship is the living God, and it is to Him we should direct our worship. As the Westminster Shorter Catechism declares so succinctly: "What is the chief end of man? The chief end of man is to glorify God, and to enjoy Him forever."

Those who have tasted the presence of the living God in true worship know that nothing can ever replace the substance of a passionate encounter with Him. If we have strayed, let's refocus onto Him, the One who alone deserves to be on the audience side of worship. Look, for instance, at the way Psalm 100 calls us to focus on God:

> Shout joyfully to the LORD, all the earth.
> Serve the LORD with gladness;
> Come before Him with joyful singing.
> Know that the LORD Himself is God;
> It is He who has made us, and not we ourselves;
> We are His people and the sheep of His pasture.
>
> Enter His gates with thanksgiving
> And His courts with praise.
> Give thanks to Him, bless His name.
> For the LORD is good;
> His lovingkindness is everlasting
> And His faithfulness to all generations.

Who is the focus of every line of this great psalm? God, the audience of One. He is the One that we praise. He is the One we adore. Biblical worship is not about *us* at all. It is all about God. And so the essential question for us when we pause to praise and worship God is this: Are our hearts and minds focused in a Godward direction?

3. What Is the Content of Worship?

Knowing the purpose and focus of worship can help us fill in the content of worship. Everything we do should be pregnant with praise and adoration for the One who has given us life and called us into a relationship with Himself. Quoting from the Westminster Shorter Catechism again:

> There is in God all that may draw forth both wonder and delight; there is a constellation of all beauties; he is *prima causa* [the first cause], the original and spring-head of being, who sheds a glory upon the creature. We glorify God when we are God-admirers; admire his attributes, which are the glistening beams by which the divine nature shines forth; his promises which are the charter of free grace, and the spiritual cabinet where the pearl of price is hid; the noble effects of his power and wisdom in making the world, which is called "the work of his fingers." Psalm 8:3. To glorify God is to have God-admiring thoughts; to esteem him most excellent, and search for diamonds in this rock only.[2]

The content of worship will "draw forth wonder and delight" as we remember God's attributes, the character qualities that describe God's nature and person and reveal the reasons He is worthy of our praise. Some of these "glistening beams" of God's diamond-like attributes are:

- *God is infinite and eternal*—Though God created time and space and can operate within both, He is not bound by time and space in the same way we are. In other words, there is no end to God. He never runs out of ideas. He's never too busy or too tired to listen to your prayers. He doesn't grow weary of your repeated confessions. He can always come to your rescue.

• *God is personal*—He can both know us and be known by us. The God of the Bible is not a mere force or fate but God with a face. Because of what Christ has accomplished, we can have a personal relationship with God that includes responsibilities and expectations on both sides.

• *God is sovereign over all*—The unique King of kings and the Lord of all creation is in charge of all that occurs both in His kingdom at large and in our small, sometimes insignificant-feeling lives.

• *God is holy*—God is free from all moral impurity. He is faithful, true, and trustworthy. He has no bias or prejudice.

• *God is omnipotent, omniscient, and omnipresent*—These "omni" attributes mean that God is all-powerful, capable of doing anything that can be done. He is all-knowing and all-wise, aware of everything you and I are going through at any point in time. He is present everywhere and is therefore able both to hear our prayers and to come to our aid.

• *God is both transcendent and immanent*—He is both far above us and is at the same time nearby, which is why we call Him the "almighty Father." As Michael Williams put it, God is always acting as both Father and King in every part of His creation.

• *God is righteous and just*—As King, God is the Lawgiver and Judge of all. He exercises this authority with impartiality and complete justice.

• *God is good and generous*—He loves and cares about all who call on His name. He is patient, compassionate, and merciful in His treatment of the poor in spirit.

In worship we take the time to come before God and praise Him for who He is and also for what He has done. We overflow with thanksgiving in our hearts that He has created each of us and everything else in the entire universe. We thank Him for loving us and sending Christ to die for our sins. We thank Him that Christ rose from the dead and, in doing so, destroyed the power and permanence of death. We thank Him for sending the Holy Spirit to live inside each of us, convicting us of our sin, convincing us of the truth, encouraging us to press on, and conforming us to the likeness of Christ.

In worship we honor God's holiness as we express our repentance and confess our sins. Or, we may sit in silence, simply waiting for Him to speak to our hearts. We recognize our total dependence on Him for wisdom and guidance, for health and wholeness, for opportunities to work and play.

4. What Are the Results of Worship?

Perhaps the best test of any efforts made are the results that follow. William Temple offered this insight, suggesting that the results of true worship are comprehensive:

> Worship is the submission of all our nature to God. It is the quickening of conscience by His holiness; the nourishment of mind with His truth; the purifying of imagination by His beauty; the opening of the heart to His love; the surrender of will to His purpose—and all of this gathered up in adoration, the most selfless emotion of which our nature is capable and therefore the chief remedy for that self-centeredness which is our original sin and the source of all actual sin. [3]

Worship involves our entire person: the conscience, the mind, the imagination, the heart, the body, and the will. When we refocus our attention from ourselves to God, when our hearts and minds begin to commune with Him, then our doubts, fears, and failures fade to the background, often to the point of insignificance. Like the storm that Jesus calmed with just a word, our struggles and striving are hushed. We are reminded that God is on His throne, that He is the King of kings and Lord of lords.

As we draw near to God, submitting ourselves to Him, His Majesty stoops, embraces us, and restores us. We are His child. He wraps us in the robe of His grace, and like the prodigal son's father, He proves Himself to be more generous to us than our highest hopes. The darkness of our doubt is burned away in the light of His presence. Our fears dissolve into the quiet confidence of surrender and trust. The embarrassment of our failures is swept away in the tide of His forgiveness.

To have such an encounter with the living God, to commune with Him in the deepest recesses of our being, to fall at His feet in honor of His Lordship and kneel before His throne—this is to worship in spirit and in truth. Just like Mary of Bethany did.

- *Does God really have a plan for my life?*
- *How can we know God's will for our lives?*
- *What does God want from us and for us?*
- *How can we recognize God's voice when He speaks to us?*

11

Hearing:

How can I recognize God's voice when He speaks to me?

I want what God wants, that's why I am so merry.

St. Francis of Assisi

I DON'T USUALLY LIKE TO START A CHAPTER off with a personal confession or a controversial statement. But the fact of the matter is, what I'm about to say may shock some of the men reading this book. However, what may shock those men may offer great joy and hope to some women, so I'm going to say it anyway:

I have, on several occasions, stopped to ask for directions.

There. I feel better. And perhaps by my setting this example, others will have the courage to admit they also don't instinctively know how to get to virtually anywhere on the planet.

Guys, listen, once you break the ice on this, once you stop and ask for directions for the very first time, trust me, it does get easier. After a while, you don't even think twice about it.

You may get so used to it that it becomes second nature for you. You might even find yourself stopping to ask for directions so often that it becomes annoying to your wife and other family members.

When you stop and think about it, asking for directions makes a lot of sense. How many times have you found yourself driving 20 or 30 minutes in the wrong direction, then having to endure the embarrassment and humiliation of turning around and being late? If you'll just go ahead and take the plunge, and ask for directions, you'll find the trade-off is really worth it. You'll save gas, time, *and* face. There's just nothing like a good set of detailed directions to help you get where you're going.

Spiritual Directions

The journey of the Christian life is similar to a road trip, in that every day is a new adventure and we often find ourselves needing to ask God for some direction. Most of us have struggled with questions like, Where is my life going? What does God want me to do with my life? Which college or university should I go to? Where should I live? Should I take this job offer? Should I marry this person? We pray, hoping God will give us some guidance as we grapple with the life-changing consequences of the various answers to these questions. We also look to God for direction as we wrestle with the complex moral and ethical choices of life that we encounter in family relationships, sexuality, citizenship, difficult medical decisions we sometimes have to make, and the managing of our financial responsibilities.

The longer we're on the planet, the more we have to face these kinds of issues, and the more our journey of life requires a strong sense of spiritual direction. The fact is, life is full of surprising twists and turns, and there are times when we can lose all sense of direction. For believers, it isn't just an option to stop and ask God for directions, it's a necessity. We admit we can't see all sides of every situation. We recognize our need for God's guidance and wisdom in the issues of real life. Being able to search out God's perspective is crucial in learning to make correct and confident decisions.

Which brings me to the main idea I want to deal with in this chapter: How can we come to know the will of God for our lives? How can we tell when God is leading us to do something or telling us not to do it? Is there a way to know when it is God's voice we are hearing?

Old Testament Examples

Both the Old and New Testaments reveal that God has been in the guidance business for quite some time. How did God communicate to the people we read about in the Bible? How did they know what His will was? Let's look at just a few examples.

A Wife for Isaac

In Genesis 24 we read that Abraham sent one of his servants to find a wife for his son Isaac from among his extended family. Now I don't know how that sounds to you, but I'm glad that's not the way we do it today. I don't even trust people to buy clothes for me, much less pick out a wife. However, that's the way they did things back then, and the good news for Isaac was Abraham promised the servant that an angel of the Lord would "go before him" or guide him in the entire endeavor. While this servant knew in advance what his goal was, he didn't know the details of how he was going to accomplish the task. He would have to begin in faith, trusting that God would guide him all along the way.

God was faithful, and He led the servant to the city of Nahor, to the town well. The servant prayed and asked the Lord to identify the right woman for him by having her offer to draw water for his camels. Before he had even finished saying that prayer, a young woman named Rebekah came along and did just that. In a beautiful tapestry of providential guidance and careful arranging of circumstances, God showed the servant that Rebekah was the one to become Isaac's wife, the love of his life.

Isn't this the way God leads us sometimes? It's not that we hear a thunderous voice from heaven or see some message written across the sky. But through a combination of prayer, guidance, and circumstances, sometimes very quietly, the Lord leads us to the people, places, and things He wants us to encounter.

The Children of Israel in the Desert

Another example of the way God spoke to His people and gave them direction is when the entire nation of Israel was led by God out of Egypt. First, God arranged their release from Pharaoh. Then He led them across the Red Sea and through the desert for 40 years. Then God led them across the Jordan River and on into the Promised Land. We are told of the many ways God led His people all along the way, sometimes in even the most minute details of their journey. He led them with a pillar of cloud during the day and a pillar of fire at night. God led them by speaking through Moses, by dreams and visions, and by other means. Many times the Israelites had to be ready to move out with little or no notice, which required paying very close attention to the signs of God's leading.

The Israelites didn't always understand what God was up to, and they didn't always like the direction in which God was leading them. Instead of trusting God, they grumbled at God. Instead of being thankful that God had set them free from the slavery of Egypt, they complained about where God was leading them, they muttered about the food He was providing for them, and they whined about the conflicts they had to go through with the surrounding nations, even though God had guaranteed that He would give them victory over those nations.

Does any of that sound familiar to you? Have you ever had difficulty understanding what God was up to? Have you ever thought that God wasn't leading your life in a very good direction, and certainly not in the one you would prefer? I have, and I suspect if you have too, we probably aren't alone. Hindsight has always offered a better perspective. God always shows Himself better than I am at making wise decisions for me. As Eugene Petersen has pointed out, the life of faith isn't meant for tourists, it's meant for pilgrims. Tourists want to hurry up and get there so they can see the sights and the show. Pilgrims are on a journey, and they're in it for the long haul.

Learning the Hard Way

After many years of guiding them through the wilderness, God finally led the children of Israel into the Promised Land. But just before He did, He sat them down and told them to remember a few things. He lovingly explained that His intention was never just to hurry up and get them there. He had guided them through the wilderness with a purpose in mind. He did it the way He did it for a reason. He wanted to bring about spiritual growth in their lives, and the reason they had to wander in the wilderness for so long was that they just weren't ready to enter the Promised Land yet. God knew the trials, temptations, and perils that awaited them there. He knew how their faith would be tested, but they didn't have a clue about it, and what's worse, some of them didn't care. They just wanted to hurry up and get there.

In Deuteronomy 8:2-3, God spoke through Moses to the people and said,

> You shall remember all the way which the LORD your God has led you in the wilderness these forty years, that He might humble you, testing you, to know what was in your heart, whether you would keep His commandments or not. He humbled you and let you be hungry, and fed you with manna which you did not

know, nor did your fathers know, that He might make
you understand that man does not live by bread alone,
but man lives by everything that proceeds out of the
mouth of the LORD.

It's pretty clear that the Lord was working on the character
and faith of His people as He led them through the wilderness.
They were proud and needed to become humble. They were
disobedient and needed to be trained through testing. They
were self-reliant and needed to learn how to trust in God.

I'm not one to pick on others who appear to be stubbornly
thickheaded in the same way I am. You know, stones and glass
houses? It's easy to look back several thousand years and point
the finger at the children of Israel for their impatience, disobedience, whining, and lack of faith. But in reality, I'm not in
despair from disconnectedness like they were. I don't have the
sunburned forehead, dried-out, cracked lips, sand-filled
clothing, or dusty, worn-out feet. However, I think we could all
learn from their experience by asking ourselves how we
respond to our times in "the wilderness." We need to recognize
how much we grumble and how little we trust God when our
life seems to be wandering around in circles. And we need to
ask ourselves this: Might God be using this time to develop a
mature character and faith in us? Might God be training our
ears to hear His voice?

New Testament Examples

The New Testament also shows us examples of God's leading
and guiding. Jesus was *"led up by the Spirit* into the wilderness
to be tempted by the devil" (Matthew 4:1). It sounds odd to say
that the Spirit would lead anyone to be tempted, but this was
indeed God's will, so that Jesus could experience all that we
experience, sympathize with us, and successfully resist temptation as a human being. Having done so without failure, He
could also help us with the temptations we must endure
(Hebrews 2:18; 4:15).

Luke tells us that during Paul's second missionary journey, "they passed through the Phrygian and Galatian region, *having been forbidden by the Holy Spirit* to speak the word in Asia; and when they had come to Mysia, they were trying to go into Bithynia, and *the Spirit of Jesus did not permit them*" (Acts 16:6-7). For Paul and his group, this was a reverse form of being led by the Spirit. Rather than leading them to do something, the Spirit prevented them from doing something. He prevented them from preaching in Asia and from going to Bithynia.

We aren't told exactly how the Spirit prevented Paul and his companions from doing those things, but looking back on it, Luke clearly recognized that it was God who had steered them away from what would have been some very logical things for them to do. In this case, it wasn't that they were being tempted to sin, it just wasn't God's will for them to preach in the province of Asia or to go to Bithynia at that time.

God has His plans and we don't always understand them. At times He may keep us from things we think would be good for us or even for His kingdom. But remember, God is working with and balancing an entire universe full of lives and events, and sometimes He holds us back for reasons we won't know until we all get home. The goal for us is to remain spiritually alert, with "ears to hear" and "eyes to see" which direction the Lord is leading us in and how we can best follow His lead.

If we're really interested in this kind of life, a life where we turn away from our self-centeredness and throw ourselves in reckless abandon onto God's will, the question then becomes, How do we know *when* we are being led by the Spirit of God? There are so many voices that vie for attention in our lives. How do we distinguish between the voice of God and all the other voices in our lives?

Learning to Listen

When I was a high school student, my family lived in Falls Church, Virginia, in a little Cape Cod-style house at the corner of Wayne and Westmoreland Roads. My older brother Larry and I shared the upstairs part of the house, which was a long, narrow attic turned into two bedrooms and a bath with slanted ceilings on both sides. My room was on the south wall, and as it is with most high school students, my room was my kingdom. This ten-by-nine private universe was where I grew up. It was where I talked for hours on the phone with my buddies and, eventually, with a girlfriend or two. It was where I sang along with Three Dog Night, the Eagles, and Chicago at the top of my lungs. I kept all my stuff up there: my guitar, comic books, a spare tire, a bowling pin. I decorated as I pleased, including a poster of two scuba divers surrounded by colorful fish, all posed under water as if looking right at me through a glass window into my room.

My room was also where I read my Bible, thought about God, and prayed about His will for my life. Many times I asked God to guide me and show me what He wanted me to do in various situations.

There was a little desk in my room where I used to do my homework in the late afternoon and early evenings. I was one of those kids who had to have several forms of stimulation going at one time. So, after school I'd sit up there with the television on and the stereo blasting at the same time while I was trying to memorize the capitals of each country in Europe.

While I was doing my late afternoon studying, Mom would be preparing dinner downstairs in the kitchen. As I moved from Geography to History, and rocked along with "Hotel California," I found a sense of security in the smell of roast beef and Yorkshire pudding that silently wound its way up through the ventilation system.

Once dinner was ready, Mom would call out, "Jimmy, come on down, dinner's ready!" In most households, she would have been audible a couple of rooms away. But because I had the music up so loud, I usually wasn't even aware she had called me. Over the next few minutes Mom would call out a couple more times, once even going to the bottom of the stairs and shouting up the stairwell, to no avail. And so most nights she'd end up resorting to a more primitive means of communicating. Mom would make a tight fist, then wind up and pound on the wall three times, just below where my room was.

Though I didn't intend to avoid hearing Mom's voice, nonetheless I couldn't hear it because I was so distracted with other things. When she took a less subtle approach to get my attention, I finally got the message.

Pop-psychologist types might misread Mom's pounding on the wall as repressed anger or a new variety of primal scream, but I knew better. She didn't pound on the wall out of anger at me, but out of love for me, knowing that I needed to come downstairs and eat my dinner.

It's that way with God sometimes. We get so preoccupied with our own pursuits, so obsessed with the things we think are important, that we just don't hear the voice of the Lord when He calls us to tell us it's time to focus on something else.

Beyond Just Seeing or Hearing

If we want to be led by God's Spirit, we must not make the mistake of thinking that our physical ears will always tell us the whole story. We can hear some things with our physical ears, but if we are to hear God, we must also listen with our spiritual ears.

The prophet Isaiah described the Messiah's ability to hear with spiritual ears:

> *The Spirit of the LORD will rest on Him,*
> *The spirit of wisdom and understanding,*
> *The spirit of counsel and strength,*
> *The spirit of knowledge and the fear of the LORD.*
> *And He will delight in the fear of the LORD,*
> *And He will not judge by what His eyes see,*
> *Nor make a decision by what His ears hear.*

Isaiah 11:2-3

Jesus, the promised Messiah, didn't judge only by what His physical eyes saw or His physical ears heard. Instead, He had the Spirit of the Lord resting on Him, which gave Him all the necessary wisdom, understanding, counsel, strength, knowledge, and fear of the Lord He needed to help Him fulfill His calling. That's how He was able to perceive the thoughts and intentions of the Pharisees, the rich young ruler, the disciples, and the many other people He encountered. Jesus could perceive things far beyond what His physical eyes could see and His physical ears could hear.

While nobody I know can equal Jesus in His awareness of what's going on in the minds and hearts of others, it does seem clear that Jesus expects those who follow Him to use more than just their physical senses when they're learning to hear what God says. In Mark 8:17-18, Jesus was trying to point this out to His disciples: "Do you not yet see or understand? Do you have a hardened heart? Having eyes, do you not see? And having ears, do you not hear?" Notice how the mind, the heart, and the will all seem to be involved here. Spiritual perception requires a willingness to hear and an open mind to learn and understand what God may be saying to us. As David Clyde Jones has said, "The will of God must be discerned through a whole-souled engagement of heart and mind and will."

Recognizing God's Voice

I have a friend who I talk with on the phone from time to time. We used to disguise our voices and try to fool each other into thinking we were an auto mechanic with bad news, a pizza place confirming an order, or a lottery commission checking on a winning ticket. After a while we grew tired of that game and started racing to see who could identify the other's voice the most quickly. My friend was fast. I went from saying "Bobby, this is Jim Thomas" to "Bobby, this is Jim" to "Bobby, this is" to "Bobby" to "Buh," and now we've got it down to where we can identify each other's voices with single-syllable grunts. Over time, we've trained our ears to be able to recognize each other's voices without much being said.

Learning to recognize the subtle voice of God is not always easy. Most of us were a whole lot better at it when we were younger. We were so teachable, we had willing hearts, we had minds much more open to that sense of wonder and astonishment that comes with communing with God. In his book *Between the Dreaming and the Coming True,* my friend Robert Benson tells the story of a four-year-old girl who was overheard whispering in her newborn baby brother's ear. "Baby," she whispers, "tell me what God sounds like. I am starting to forget."[1] She was just four, and already she was starting to forget. I am more than ten times that. Sometimes the silence is deafening.

Maybe that's what Jesus meant when He said, "Truly I say to you, unless you are converted and become like children, you will not enter the kingdom of heaven" (Matthew 18:3). At the time, Jesus was talking to some adults who had been arguing about which of them would be the greatest in the kingdom of heaven. In other words, they were acting childish, but Jesus wanted them to become childlike. The difference determines whether or not a person can hear God's voice.

The older we get, the more voices we lend our ears to. Some of them are yelling, others are talking, some are like background noise, and some barely whisper. There are the voices of culture, the voices of our family, the voices of our doubts and fears. There are the voices of our pain, our anger, our guilt, and our greed. We all have a cacophony of voices inside our heads, simultaneously hurling summons for us to "remember this" and "watch out for that." If we forget how to distinguish God's voice from all these other voices, we can drown in the din as we thrash about, trying to hear what God might be saying and how He might be leading us.

Fortunately, God doesn't leave it all up to us. He takes the initiative to cut through the chaos and speak to the hearts and minds of those who truly want to hear from Him. The voice of the Holy Spirit is far from mute. If He needs to, He too can pound on a wall. When He wants to get your attention, He will, even if your ears are distracted.

God Speaks—Through the Scriptures

Throughout the Bible we find God speaking in a variety of ways. Sometimes He spoke directly to an individual, sometimes through a prophet, sometimes through visions and dreams. But many of the great people of faith did what they believed was the will of God without a lot of fireworks or theater. They just made their decision based on what they already knew God would want them to do. If they had a question about something, they knew they could hear God's voice as they read the ancient Scriptures.

In one Old Testament passage we read: "How can a young man keep his way pure? By keeping it according to Your word. With all my heart I have sought You; do not let me wander from Your commandments. Your word I have treasured in my heart, that I may not sin against You" (Psalm 119:9-11). In another we find, "Your word is a lamp to my feet, and a light to my path" (Psalm 119:105). And in the New Testament we are told this: "All Scripture is inspired by God and profitable for teaching, for reproof, for correction, for training in righteousness; so that the man of God may be adequate, equipped for every good work" (2 Timothy 3:16-17).

These passages make some amazing claims about God's Word, the book we call the Bible. Notice how practical God's Word claims to be. It helps us keep our way pure, it helps us resist temptation and sin, it is a lamp to our feet and a light to our path in life. The Word of God is useful for giving us guidance, for correcting us when we go wrong, and for training us about how to remain faithful to God.

If you are trying to hear the voice of God, remember this: God will not contradict His Word. In the pages of the Bible we have a vast array of resources to guide us along the way. As

David Clyde Jones has pointed out,[2] within the Scriptures there are clear mandates in the form of negative prohibitions and positive commands, and there are also indications of permission and general counsel. Further, there are examples that show a precedent and reveal how God's laws were applied in a given situation in history. All of this helpful information is available to those who prayerfully give themselves to the study of God's Word.

If there is not a clear mandate in Scripture that addresses the issue you are struggling with, you should look for a more general, guiding principle or piece of counsel. There may be an example of permission, a precedent, or an expression of approval from Scripture that will help you hear God's voice. Once you find a passage you feel speaks to your situation, then prayerfully consider how you should apply it in your life.

God's voice is heard most clearly and directly through the pages of Scripture. If you have trouble interpreting or applying what is being said in the Scriptures, get some help from a fellow believer who is experienced in God's Word, or from some of the resources for interpreting and applying the message of the Bible that I mentioned in the chapter titled "Learning."

God Speaks—Through Prayer

Most people think of prayer as "talking to God." I think we miss one of the primary purposes of prayer if we limit it to that. Prayer is the venue in which we move from communication *to* God to communion *with* God. In the stillness and quiet of that deep communion, the voice of God's Spirit can speak to us. As I said before, God's voice has never been audible to me, but there have been times when it was clear to me. What is audible speaks only to my physical ears, but God's voice speaks to the ears of my heart. Prayer is the training ground where the ears of my heart learn how to distinguish the voice of God from all the other voices in my life.

William Barclay said it well:

> Prayer is not a way of making use of God; prayer is a way of offering ourselves to God in order that He should be able to make use of us. It may be that one of our great faults in prayer is that we talk too much and listen too little. When prayer is at its highest, we wait in silence for God's voice to us; we linger in His presence for His peace and His power to flow over us and around us; we lean back in His everlasting arms and feel the serenity of perfect security in Him.[3]

God Speaks—Through Others

Another way God speaks to us is through the counsel of others. When I'm looking for guidance on something that the Scriptures don't address directly, if I'm not sure what to do, I'll ask for counsel from several close friends and family members who are spiritually mature and who have shown themselves to be wise in the ways of the faith.

By this, I don't mean I have some friends whose highest wish for me is that I will get everything I think I want out of life. That's not what I look for in a close friend. I look for people who are intentionally engaged in the pursuit of God themselves, who, when they say they will pray for me, aren't talking about "sending positive thoughts my way." The kind of friends I mean are the ones who take God seriously and believe that I should do the same. They see themselves as part of the unfolding kingdom of God and understand that this means we are all in the service of our King.

We share a passionate allegiance to that same King and are committed to seeing each other grow in character, in faith, and in purity. Sometimes that kind of servanthood must include sacrifice. Sometimes it includes costs, inconveniences, suffering, and pain. But through it all we have the permission to speak into each other's lives to encourage, to challenge, to advise and admonish.

As Proverbs 27:17 says, "Iron sharpens iron, so one man sharpens another." To sharpen each other, we cannot engage in politeness and pleasantry all the time. There is by necessity some heat and friction, but there is always the motive of love for the other person. With a motive of love, there is room for trust and open discussion. This provides the maximum opportunity for God to speak through each of us to the other.

God Speaks—Through Circumstances

In the summer after my first year at college, my life was in a state of limbo. I had not had a good first year academically. I wasn't prepared for the distractions of autonomous living and ended up having to move back home. I wasn't sure what I was supposed to do with my life, and I felt like I was just treading water.

Then one day I got a call from a guy who introduced himself as the new youth director at the church my family attended. I didn't know who he was because, frankly, I hadn't been to church recently. My spiritual life was on the back burner with the temperature set on "Low."

He told me his name was Jerry Schneider, and he wanted to know whether I would come and serve as the lifeguard at River Valley Ranch (aka RVR), where the church had always taken the youth group for a week of summer camp. He'd heard that I had my lifeguard's certification and that I liked going up to RVR, and so that was the reason he thought of calling me. Jerry also mentioned that they needed a recreation person to handle the sports and wondered whether my best friend Rick would be interested in coming along and helping out as well.

I had to admit, the offer of a free week at camp did sound pretty good. But as I look back on it now, my initial response to Jerry must have seemed a little cold. I told him we might be interested if we could both get off work from our summer jobs, the one condition being that he would assure us we wouldn't have any kind of spiritual responsibilities. I confessed to him that I was working through some things and just didn't feel like I was in the right frame of mind to be a spiritual leader to anyone else. Jerry understood and said that he appreciated my honesty. He agreed to the condition, and a few weeks later I was on my way back to RVR.

I had been to the ranch as a camper for eight years in a row when I was younger, so when I pulled onto the grounds, it brought back a flood of memories. Horseback rides, rodeo shows, hayrides, puppy-love romances, goofy skits, sing-alongs, testimonies and s'mores at the campfire, the whole she-bang. I loved my times as a kid up at RVR, and it was a great feeling to be back there again.

Rick and I were assigned to a newly remodeled, private bunkhouse where we'd be able to get a good night's sleep. Rick took our stuff down there while I went up to the pool to get familiar with the new chlorination system. After looking it over, then stowing my whistle, trunks, and towel in a locker, I headed back down to the registration office to check in with Jerry.

Unexpected News

When he saw me approaching, Jerry's face displayed one of those half-wince-half-smiles that told me he was about to ask me to do a huge favor, which is precisely what happened next. It seemed that not one, but both of the junior high boys' counselors had canceled at the last minute, one for business reasons, the other because of a bad cold. Jerry had nowhere to turn but to me and Rick. Everyone else had been assigned as counselors elsewhere, and there were 20 seventh- and eighth-grade boys who needed someone to bunk with them every night and lead them in devotions each morning.

Reluctantly, we retrieved our sleeping bags from the new and "sure to be quiet" bunkhouse and moved into the run-down and "sure to be run over" boys' cabin. In reality I wasn't so much worried about the lack of sleep as I was scared to death about the morning devotions. Coming up with something meaningful to say about God to twenty 13- and 14-year old boys was frightening, especially when my own spiritual life had been so flat.

That afternoon I decided on a strategy. I would just do what I had seen done when I was a junior high camper. The next morning, I opened the Bible to the book of John, read a portion out loud and then proceeded to tell them what I thought it meant. Next we went around in a circle and shared prayer requests, and then went back around again until everyone had had a chance to pray.

It's true what they say about the Bible—it's not just about information, it's also about transformation. And that's exactly what happened to me and my friend Rick that week at River Valley Ranch. As our "stay up all night laughing and making weird sounds" junior high boys' cabin read the Bible together each morning, we heard from God. As we prayed together, we talked to God. And while we were doing those two things, God broke through to us in a brand new way. My faith was renewed, and I now mark that week as a watershed experience in my life.

Jerry was a good youth director, but he didn't mastermind the whole thing in hopes of renewing my spiritual life. He just needed a lifeguard and a recreation director. The two counselors who canceled had, and still have, no idea that their schedules had to be changed so that Rick and I would be asked to take their place. God had planned it all. He had put a divine appointment on my calendar, and it was that I would spend the week with 20 short-attention-spanned junior highers, eating meals, wrestling, playing football, singing songs, laughing until all hours of the night, and yes, studying the Bible and praying together.

Guidance comes to us in many ways, and one of them is when God comes after you, rearranges your schedule, takes you out of your comfort zone to get your attention, and then shows you how much He loves you...even when you've not been loving Him very well. Because God rearranged the circumstances in my life, He got my attention again, and my spiritual life was refreshed and renewed.

But wait, that's not the end of this story.

God's Multiple Plans

One night in the dining hall during that same week at camp, Rick brought someone over to meet me. She was a skinny little blond girl who was a bit perky but not in an unattractive way. She had a light in her brown eyes that said she knew what it meant to be in love with life. It seems that she was having "boy trouble" that week, and she needed someone older and wiser to talk to, someone who could help her understand what God might be trying to say to her. Why Rick would have thought to bring her to me remains a mystery to this day. (Well, maybe not. Read on.)

To make a long story short, I spent some time talking with her and tried to help her understand as much as I could about the male psyche. I apologized for the thickheadedness, selfishness, and insensitivity my gender often displays. I assured her that God was watching out for her and would help her through this difficult time. We prayed together, and that week she and I became good friends. Over the next few years we got closer, driving to church together and talking, sometimes for hours, over the phone. Her name was Kim Wright, and today she has been my best friend and wife for more than 23 years.

Are You Ready to Hear Him?

The voice of God can be heard in many ways, and one of them is when God moves you into just the right place at just the right time. When that happens, if you aren't asleep at the wheel, if you have "eyes to see" and "ears to hear," you might just find something He wants you to find. During that one week of my life, because of God's guidance, I was reacquainted with the Lord of my life and met up with the love of my life.

In guiding us, God may choose to shut an open door or open a shut door. He may lead us to do something or prevent us from doing something. God may change the outcome of some project you thought was a done deal. God may alter the cooperation of others, He might supply the funds you thought were impossible to get, He may rearrange your calendar in ways you could never have imagined.

But the thing to remember is this: God is not limited to speaking to us in just one way. He will likely confirm His will by speaking to us in more than just one way. He is not trying to hide His will from us, He works hard to make sure we know what He wants.

We do well when we remain open to hearing from God however He may choose to communicate with us. As Dallas Willard puts it, "We must be open to the possibility of God's addressing us in whatever way he chooses, or else we may walk right past a burning bush."

Perhaps we pass by "burning bushes" all the time because they aren't the way we expect them to be. Maybe they're not as blatant and obvious as we think they ought to be, and while we're busy looking for incendiary signs, Jesus is quietly waiting for us to simply trust Him and walk the walk of faith. Maybe the answer we've been looking for is to be found on the next page we'll turn to in His book, or in listening through the quiet, on our knees. It might be in the "chance" meeting of an old friend at a coffeehouse, who reminds you of something you used to know full well but you have since forgotten.

Are you ready to become childlike again? Do you have your ears inclined toward heaven? Are you living your life in anticipation of hearing from God? He is ready to speak. Are you ready to listen?

- *What does God want us to become?*
- *Does God want the same thing for everyone?*
- *Why are we alive?*
- *What does spiritual growth look like?*

12

Becoming:
What does it take to grow spiritually?

> Grace is never a stationary thing, it is always found in a becoming.
>
> *Meister Eckhart*

WHEN I WAS A LITTLE KID I JUST COULDN'T WAIT to grow up. I looked forward to the days when I would be just like the "big" people. I wanted to drive a car, get married, have a checking account, and not have to clean my plate at every meal. There was something exciting about growing up. Even though I knew it didn't happen all at once, I looked forward to getting the process started.

Christian spirituality also involves a desire to grow up. The Christian journey is a life in motion because it is always a life of growth. This is no static spirituality! In a word, Christian spirituality is a "becoming."

It all starts when we become a Christian by accepting Christ as our Lord and Savior. At that time, God deals with the legal problem of our sin by wiping the slate clean. God forgives us for our sin based on the things done by Christ, who died on the cross in our place. The Bible calls this *justification by faith*, and it is the one-time, once-and-for-all work of Christ on our behalf. But then our spiritual growth continues as the Holy Spirit transforms our daily lives and gives us power over temptation and sin. This day-to-day working out of our salvation is an ongoing process that the Bible calls *sanctification*, which means "to set apart," or "to make holy." As God changes our hearts, step by step and bit by bit, we see the fruit of the Spirit's work in our life.

Francis Schaeffer expressed it this way: "But after we become Christians, the moments proceed, the clock continues to tick; and in every moment of time, our calling is to believe God, raise the empty hands of faith, and let fruit flow out through us." In raising the empty hands of faith, we humbly recognize that it is God who is at work in us, both to will and to work for His good pleasure. God provides the power, our part is to turn to Him and receive what He offers.

But we must not make the mistake of thinking we are passive in our spiritual growth. Our faith requires nurture and maintenance on our part. It is not just the acknowledgment of correct doctrine. A growing faith is built upon the foundation of God's Word, empowered by the Holy Spirit, and then put into practice as a matter of the will and disposition. As Christian ethicist David Clyde Jones has said: "The real problem of ethics is not in finding the rule to direct us how to glorify and enjoy God but in having the will to make this our aim in the first place." Are we aiming at spiritual growth? Do we truly desire to glorify and enjoy God?

This principle of the involvement of the will is seen in a wonderful old poem:

> *One ship drives east and another drives west*
> *With the selfsame winds that blow;*
> *'Tis the set of the sails*
> *And not the gales*
> *Which tells us the way to go.*

Ella Wheeler Wilcox

So, let me ask you: In which direction are your spiritual sails set? Setting our sails means living intentionally, fixing our course. If we are to grow spiritually, a couple of things will be required from us. First, the direction of a sailing ship is controlled by the rudder as it turns in one direction or another. You can turn a ship in such a direction that will allow it to catch the wind in its sails, you can try to sail against the wind, or you can simply tie up the sails and lie adrift.

Turning the ship of our lives into the wind of God's Spirit means putting ourselves in the path of God's grace. This includes carving out time to fill our hearts and minds with the Word of God and to commune with God in prayer, confessing our sins and receiving God's forgiveness daily. It includes making time for worshiping God, serving God and others, and being with God's people. Through these and other spiritual disciplines, the life of the spirit is nurtured and encouraged to grow.

These are not once-for-all efforts. You don't just accept Christ and then forget about it. We need to commit ourselves to practicing the spiritual disciplines on a regular basis. We need to be filled and refilled with the Spirit over and over again because, frankly, we leak. But God is rich in grace, and His mercies are new every morning. Our daily prayer can be "Lord, fill me with your Spirit once again." God provides the power for motion, we turn into the wind of the Spirit, and He fills us, enabling us to follow where He leads us.

The Desire to Want What God Wants

I live in Nashville, Tennessee, aka "Music City, USA." In addition to being the home of country music, this town is also considered the hub of activity for contemporary Christian music. As you might imagine, there are a lot of Christians who are songwriters and musicians who have come to Nashville. Some of them moved here because they thought God wanted them to. They believed that God had gifted them and was going to use their musical endeavors somehow, so they headed off to the place that seems to be the center for that kind of activity.

There are also a few people who moved here because they thought God told them He was going to make them big-time recording stars. It's not that they run around saying it out loud all the time, it's more latent. Yet somehow, they believe they've heard a spiritual calling to become a "Christian" version of a superstar celebrity, complete with all the fame and fortune the Christian music business has to offer.

This reminds me of the times I used to say jokingly that I thought God was calling me to start a ministry in some exotic vacation spot like Hawaii or the south of France. I've tried to find examples of those kinds of ministry callings in Scripture, you know, to justify what I wanted to do, but I haven't been able to find any yet. (If you know where they are, please do let me know so I can get on with my calling and start a church on Maui or the French Riviera.)

My point is, there are people who seem to equate the ideas in their own head with the voice of God. I'm not saying there's anything wrong with wanting to pursue the dreams you have or the vocations you may be wanting to try out. That's not my point at all. But we should be honest enough not to confuse our personal ambitions with God's will. Sometimes they will be in line with each other, sometimes they will not.

Am I saying that when people pursue their own ambitions, they have misread God? Sometimes. Am I suggesting that people are completely incapable of hearing from God? No. Are we doomed to wander around in a fog about what God's will is for our lives? Not at all. But when we pray for God to reveal His will for our lives, we need to make sure we aren't really just asking Him to show us how to make more money, advance in our career, find a new boyfriend, or obtain the things *we* think will make our life more convenient, comfortable, entertaining, and fun. In regard to this, F.B. Meyer wrote, "So long as there is some thought of personal advantage, some idea of acquiring the praise and commendation of men, some aim of self-aggrandizement, it will be simply impossible to find out God's purpose concerning us."[1]

That said, we must admit that we will always have some mixture of right and wrong motives. But we are still responsible to ask the question, Do I want what God wants for my life? It's important to prayerfully check our motives when we're trying to discern God's will. Jesus gave us a guiding principle that will help: "If anyone wishes to come after Me, he must deny himself, and take up his cross and follow Me. For whoever wishes to save his life will lose it; but whoever loses his life for My sake will find it" (Matthew 16:24-25). There is a kind of ambition here. It's the ambition to follow Jesus and to "save" our life. But it is clearly not a self-centered ambition. It's an ambition filled with abandonment and allegiance, abandonment of selfishness and allegiance to Christ. It is the laying down of one's life in surrender so that we want what God wants.

Three Things We Should Want

In the Lord's Prayer we pray, "hallowed be Your name. Your kingdom come. Your will be done, on earth as it is in heaven" (Matthew 6:9-10). If we desire to be led by the Spirit, we must find ourselves wanting three things. We must be devoted to "hallowing" His name, which simply means regarding His name and His person as sacred. Instead of distorting or denigrating the name of God by the way we live, we make it our purpose to live in such a way as to honor the name of God. We must also be committed to advancing His kingdom, which is not so much a geographic kingdom as it is the reign of God in the lives of His people. It includes the idea of an ever-increasing submission to His lordship. And third, we must devote our lives to seeing His will done here on earth just as it is in heaven. This necessarily includes seeing that God's will is done in our own lives.

Anything but Dull

The apostle Paul, in a broad and sweeping statement, tells us something else about those who are being led by the Spirit: "All who are being led by the Spirit of God, these are sons of God" (Romans 8:14). This is evidence of our adoption as children of God. We find ourselves wanting, desiring, longing to be led by the Holy Spirit as we set ourselves to do the will of our Father in each immediate moment. Picking up dry cleaning, going to the post office, raking leaves, chauffeuring our children, and in relationships with everyone from our spouse to the community at large, we have the opportunity to be led by the Spirit.

Notice the word is "led." The Holy Spirit leads by persuasion, not by coercion. There is no force involved. True believers are led by the Spirit and follow joyfully because they delight in doing God's will.

I have two miniature schnauzers, a salt-and-pepper-colored one named Rose and a black one named Violet. When I walk them on leash, they pull as hard as they can, stretching the leash for all the length they can get out of it. If I were to let go of the leash, they'd be gone in a flash.

Rose and Violet don't know any better, but they remind me of the many people who call themselves Christians yet who will ask, "Can I do such-and-such a thing and still be a Christian?" Well, because we are saved by grace and not by what we do, the answer is technically "yes." Christ died for our sins, and He died for all of them, no matter how "big" or "small" we might think they are. But, setting aside the question about any individual act of sin, doesn't it seem strange that someone who says he truly desires to follow Christ would even be asking how far out on the edge he can go, or how far he can stretch the leash, and still be considered a Christian? What does that say about his spiritual disposition?

Jesus said, "I came that they may have life, and have it abundantly" (John 10:10). As we begin to want what God wants in our lives, life becomes increasingly full of surprise, it becomes the greatest of great adventures, and we are constantly refilled with astonishment and wonder. God is behind the steering wheel, and we never know precisely which way He will turn us. This is what makes the Christian faith anything but dull. Wanting what God wants requires a certain kind of reckless abandon, a passionate allegiance, and a ferocious trust.

What God Wants

So what exactly does God want? How can we know what God's goal is for our lives? The answers to those questions will help us identify when it is God who is speaking, leading, and guiding us. God wouldn't lead us into something that runs against His goal for our lives. If we are curious about whether we should do something or not, we can test the ideas we are considering to see whether they move us deeper into what God wants.

In identifying what God wants, we should distinguish between the *general* will of God and the *particular* will of God. The general will of God includes that which has been revealed for all people, at all times, everywhere. This includes what we refer to as the Ten Commandments, and it includes Jesus' summary of God's law:

> "You shall love the LORD your God with all your heart, and with all your soul, and with all your mind." This is the great and foremost commandment. The second is like it, "You shall love your neighbor as yourself." On these two commandments depend the whole Law and the Prophets (Matthew 22:37-40).

These things are what God wants from all people, at all times, everywhere.

The particular will of God deals with things such as our jobs, whether or who we should marry, where we live, and so on. I won't pretend to give you an answer to questions about God's particular will for your life, that must come from the Lord to you. You must set yourself to hear His voice as He speaks through the various means He chooses (which were discussed in the previous chapter). But I would like to emphasize that the general outlines of God's will have been revealed in Scripture, and they can often help us answer any specific questions we are wrestling with. We must commit ourselves to the *general* will of God if we want to know and be guided by the *particular* will of God. Then we can allow what is clear to help us interpret what is not yet clear.

In the record of God's creation of human beings we are given a glimpse of what God's primary goal is for all of our lives. In Genesis 1:26-27 we're told that

> God said, "Let Us make man in Our image, according to Our likeness; and let them rule over the fish of the sea and over the birds of the sky and over the cattle and over all the earth, and over every creeping thing that creeps on the earth." And God created man in His own image, in the image of God He created him; male and female He created them.

Did you notice the repeated theme, that human beings were intentionally created in the image of God? This reveals the primary goal God has for our lives. It's not about wealth or poverty, career advancement or loss of a job. It's not about academic achievement or social improvement. God wants His image to be reflected in us. What an awesome privilege! What an honor! The infinite God of all creation carefully designed each one of us to reflect His image!

Some of you might be thinking that this sounds a little odd. You look in the mirror and it makes you wonder why in the world God would want His image to be reflected in you. Why not the Grand Canyon, the Mediterranean, or the Milky Way? What about the eagle, the lion, or the antelope? Those things are awesome, beautiful, and inspiring to everyone. Why would God want to reflect His image in a plumber from South Dakota, a taxi-mom from Phoenix, or a social worker from the Bronx?

The reason is quite simple. It's because this isn't about what you look like or what you do. This is about the potential God sees in you simply because of who He made you to be and who He wants you to become.

Why You Are Alive

Christian spirituality is like a detective story, but as G.K. Chesterton says, it is a *divine* detective story. It's not so much concerned with why a person is dead, but why he or she is alive. Here is the secret that philosophers have been trying to search out for a long, long time: the one they call the *summum bonum,* or the highest good. It is the most noble pursuit, the key to fulfillment and satisfaction in life. The highest good for your life and mine is that God's image would be reflected in us.

People often ask, What's the meaning of life? Why are we alive? Do our lives have any real purpose? The Bible answers these questions by telling us that yes, we do have a purpose, and it goes far beyond punching a time card, far beyond the mundane routine of family responsibilities, far beyond our obsessions with appearance, fitness, or the approval of others. It goes far beyond the things we own and far beyond all the thrills our money can buy. The purpose of life is that we would reflect God's image! God didn't plan that for any other part of creation. All of creation declares God's glory, but only human beings reflect God's image. What a joyful opportunity we have to live extraordinary lives! Each moment of each day is pregnant with possibilities for us to reflect the image of God, wherever we go, whatever we do.

The trip to the grocery store is no longer just to get milk, soup, and cereal. We can reflect God's image as we pull into the parking lot, as we go up and down each aisle, and on to waiting in line at the checkout behind that lady with all the coupons. Answering the phone becomes an adventure of seeing how God might cause His image to be reflected through you to the person calling. Going to church is no longer about what we can get out of the worship service but about what we can bring to it as we seek to reflect God's image to those we meet there.

Once we begin to want what God wants for our lives, then we can begin learning how to become the person He wants us to become.

Becoming God's Person

A well-known young actress was once asked her opinion on smoking cigarettes. She replied, "Smoking kills. If you're killed, you've lost a very important part of your life."

Mmmmm. I suppose that's true.

There are some views of spirituality that promote the loss of another very important part of your life. They suggest that the goal of spirituality is the assimilation of your personality into the great cosmic unity, which of course requires the loss of your personality. The more spiritual you become, the more *you* disappear.

Pardon the simpleness of my question, but why would you even want to get out of bed, much less go about your daily life, if you were destined to disappear? Where is the hope for meaning in a spirituality whose primary goal is that you cease to exist and are fused into some divine version of *Star Trek*'s "Borg"?

This idea is the complete opposite of that found in Christian spirituality. The Christian faith teaches that your personality is unique, that you have real value and purpose, and that the goal of your spiritual life is not assimilation. When Christians grow spiritually, they become more and more the one-of-a-kind people God has created them to be. We aren't supposed to become mindless clones of anyone else. God created us as rational, self-aware individuals who live in dynamic relationship with our rational, self-aware Creator and with other rational, self-aware individuals.

Christian spirituality teaches that our personalities are destined for distinction, not extinction. Each of us is an original, uniquely created by God for His glory, and designed to remain that way for eternity. Nor do our personalities disappear when we die a physical death. When Jesus was on the Mount of Transfiguration, Peter, James, and John saw Him talking with two identifiable individuals who had long since died physically, Moses and Elijah. If human personality fades to nothingness when we die, Jesus wouldn't have been talking with two persons who had names.

In the New Testament book of Hebrews we read about some of the giants of the faith, men and women whose stories are told throughout the Scriptures but who died a long time ago. The author goes on to paint a word picture of those of us who are still alive on earth, describing us as if we were running the race of faith in an athletic stadium. The stands are filled with the saints who have already finished their race. They are called a "great cloud of witnesses." Though they have died physically, they still exist as distinct personalities, and because of Christ's resurrection victory over death, we will all one day rise to live with the Lord and with each other forever.

According to the Bible, while we are alive and here on earth we are supposed to be growing spiritually, becoming more and more like Christ in our character. And when you think about it, Jesus was the most fully human person to ever live. As we become more like Christ, we become more fully human too, doing what humans were originally designed to do: reflect God's image. We draw closer and closer to the Lord, not in hopes of being absorbed or assimilated, but to more accurately reflect His image by more fully becoming the person He wants us to be.

Avoiding the False You's

The *Brookesia perarmata*, otherwise known as a chameleon, looks like some kind of monster from a little child's worst nightmare. It has horns, a dorsal crest, a long and fast tongue to catch its prey, and eyes that operate independently, rotating like machine gun turrets, which allows it to see in two directions at once.

Chameleons are best known for their ability to change color. But what most people don't know is that when chameleons do change color, it's not only to match their background. They may change color because of their health or body temperature, to attract another chameleon, or to hide from a predator. And most chameleons have what is called a "rest coloration," that is, a color they revert to that is their true self.

There were times I lived my life like a human chameleon, eyes shifting, looking around in every direction, trying to see what everybody else was doing so I could adjust and fit in, and not be left out or thought poorly of. Over the years, I got pretty good at it and could change color based on whatever group I was with at the moment. I could turn on a dime to fit in with whoever I was with. But what I've discovered is, when you live your life as a social chameleon, you never have a sense of just being yourself.

I'm not saying there's anything wrong with wanting to be loved or liked. But speaking from my own experience, if we are always adjusting ourselves to win the approval of others or to hide our true selves from others, we will find ourselves either disappearing into a fog of schizophrenia or drowning in an ocean of anxiety.

God created each of us to be our unique selves, and when we focus on becoming the individuals God designed us to be, we begin to find our "rest coloration." And take it from a recovering chameleon like me, the rest is more than worth the risk.

Christian spirituality includes the call for you and me to turn away from all the false selves we might be tempted to try to become out of envy, curiosity, insecurity, or greed. God's will is never for us to become something or someone we are not. He has created each of us with a special combination of gifts, talents, and abilities that can be employed in His service and that will bring glory to His name. Don't waste time and energy trying to be somebody else. If you do that, you'll stop being *you*. And if you aren't being you, you can bet nobody else will be. When God created you, He had someone special in mind who could reflect His image in a unique way. If you don't become the person God wants you to be, the spot God created for you to fill will remain empty. In other words, be yourself. We all need you, and God wants you! Personal authenticity is a high act of worship.

We are not all the same. As a matter of fact, some of us are *very* different. My wife is perhaps the most distinctly different individual I've ever known, and she has a very unusual combination of gifts and talents. She's a highly disciplined, well-organized person, but she is also very creative. She's an author, a musician, a poet, and a painter, but she can also do the taxes! I marvel at her sometimes. It could only be an infinitely creative God who could have designed a person like Kim. She is being conformed to the likeness of Christ as she is faithful to living out who she was uniquely designed to be. And each of us can be conformed to Him in the same way.

Discovering Your Spiritual Gifts

If you've never done it, you should prayerfully identify the spiritual gifts God has given you so you can put them to use and become more the person He made you to be. In Romans 12 the apostle Paul identifies some of the gifts God gives us and offers us instruction in the attitude with which we are to put them to work.

> Since we have gifts that differ according to the grace given to us, each of is to exercise them accordingly: if prophecy, according to the proportion of his faith; if service, in his serving; or he who teaches, in his teaching; or he who exhorts, in his exhortation; he who gives, with liberality; he who leads, with diligence; he who shows mercy, with cheerfulness. Let love be without hypocrisy. Abhor what is evil; cling to what is good. Be devoted to one another in brotherly love; give preference to one another in honor; not lagging behind in diligence, fervent in spirit, serving the Lord; rejoicing in hope, persevering in tribulation, devoted to prayer, contributing to the needs of the saints, practicing hospitality (Romans 12:6-13).

Here's a pretty clear example of God's will for our lives. There's enough there to keep us busy for quite some time. Do you find yourself wanting to bring home every stray dog? Maybe you have the gift of mercy. Do you find yourself questioning the message behind every movie or TV show? Perhaps you have the gift of teaching. Do you find yourself inviting people to your house for dinner all the time? Perhaps you have the gift of hospitality. Look for yourself in this list, and ask God to show you how and where He might like you to start using your spiritual gifts.

I look at this passage and immediately find myself challenged by the humility and selfless devotion to which we are called as we put the gifts God has given us into action. Christ wants each of us to use our gifts for a purpose higher than our own self-interests. We're supposed to use these gifts to glorify God and serve our brothers and sisters. That's part of giving your life away and then finding it again.

Being Transformed

I'm usually so obsessed with my own wants and needs that I fail to focus my life on God's will or the good of others. Paul anticipates this when he tells us,

> Do not be conformed to this world, but be transformed by the renewing of your mind, so that you may prove what the will of God is, that which is good and acceptable and perfect (Romans 12:2).

"This world" says, "Look out for yourself. Take care of good ol' Number One. Climb the ladder of success, and if you have to step on a few people in the process, so be it!" But God doesn't want us to conform to that message. As Richard Foster says,

> The fruit of the Spirit is not push, drive, climb, grasp, and trample. Don't let the rat-racing world keep you on its treadmill. There is a legitimate place for blood, sweat, and tears; but it should have its roots in the call of God, not in the desire to get ahead. Life is more than a climb to the top of the heap.[2]

That climb to the top takes a lot out of a human personality. It requires so many compromises, and results in so many needless casualties. The money you make, the power you gain, the pleasure you find—these pursuits may be fine in the right context, but an obsession with them is sure to callous your soul. As comedienne Lily Tomlin put it, "The trouble with the rat race is, even if you win, you're still a rat."

I don't mean to offend you if you happen to like rats, but the truth is, rats were not created in the image of God. Paul says human beings have an opportunity to "prove what the will of God is" as His image is reflected in our transformed minds and lives. If you've been living the life of a rat, I want you to know that God has the power to change you. As you yield your heart and give your mind to renewal through the study of His Word, through prayer, and through service, God will transform you.

The word "transform" in the original Greek language of the New Testament is *metamorphoo*, from which we get our word metamorphosis. It's the word we use when we're talking about a caterpillar being transformed into a butterfly. Or, in this case, a rodent being transformed into an image-bearer of the Almighty God.

When Jesus said "If any one wishes to come after Me, let him deny himself, and take up his cross and follow Me," He wasn't talking about a denial of your personality or some kind of ascetic self-denial. If you want to follow Jesus you don't have to go live in a cave somewhere in the desert, wear wild animal skins, and eat bugs. Denying yourself means denying the self-centered part of who you are. It means living your life to the fullest for the glory of God.

You may or may not be called to write hit songs, pastor a mega-church, or become a successful actor. You may or may not be called to be a mom, a mechanic, or a construction worker. But I do know this, if you do end up doing any of those things, God wants you to do them full-on, with all you have and for His glory. If you are a songwriter, write the best songs you can write. If you are called to pastor, do so with a heart full of compassion. If God does want you to become an actor, a mom, a mechanic, or a construction worker, you can rest assured that God wants you to do those things with passion, integrity, diligence, and discipline. No matter what you do, will to do it for the glory of God, being all the person He has designed you to be.

In Christian spirituality, we answer all of the questions about what God wants us to *do* based on the answers to the questions about who God wants us to *be*. The Christian faith is about *being* before it is about *doing*. God wants you to know all the richness of life in the Spirit, a vibrant life, full of new growth.

In each chapter of this book, I've tried to describe how the life of the spirit is experienced and expressed from the Christian point of view. If you find yourself wanting to learn more, please explore some of the excellent books that I've listed in the bibliography section that follows.

May God fill you with all His fullness as you continue to draw near to Him. Lean hard into His grace. God loves you, He will strengthen you, He will help you grow, He will even supply the faith you need to believe. And remember, Christian spirituality is a lifelong process. It's all about *becoming*.

Bibliography

Benner, David. *Care of Souls: Revisioning Christian Nurture and Counsel.* Grand Rapids, MI: Baker Books, 1998.

Buechner, Frederick. *The Hungering Dark.* San Francisco: HarperSanFrancisco, 1969.

Chapell, Bryan. *Christ-Centered Preaching: Redeeming the Expository Sermon.* Grand Rapids, MI: Baker Books, 1994.

Curtis, Brent, and John Eldredge. *The Sacred Romance: Drawing Closer to the Heart of God.* Nashville, TN: Thomas Nelson, 1997.

Eldredge, John. *The Journey of Desire: Searching for the Life We've Only Dreamed Of.* Nashville, TN: Thomas Nelson, 2000.

Foster, Richard. *Celebration of Discipline: The Path to Spiritual Growth.* San Francisco: Harper & Row, 1988.

Gallup, George, Jr., and Timothy Jones. *The Next American Spirituality: Finding God in the Twenty-First Century.* Colorado Springs, CO: Victor Books, 2000.

Guinness, Os. *The Call.* Nashville, TN: Word Publishing, 1998.

Hoekema, Anthony A. *Created in God's Image.* Grand Rapids, MI: William B. Eerdmans, 1986.

Laurie, Greg. *The Upside Down Church.* Wheaton, IL: Tyndale House, 1999.

Lewis, C.S. *Mere Christianity.* New York: Macmillan, 1960.

———. *Surprised by Joy.* New York: Harcourt, Brace & World, Inc., 1955.

Manning, Brennan. *The Ragamuffin Gospel: Embracing the Unconditional Love of God.* Sisters, OR: Multnomah Publishers, 1990.

———. *Ruthless Trust: The Ragamuffin's Path to God.* San Francisco: HarperSanFrancisco, 2000.

McCartney, Dan, and Charles Clayton. *Let the Reader Understand: A Guide to Interpreting and Applying the Bible.* Wheaton, IL: Victor Books, 1994.

McGrath, Alister. *Christian Spirituality.* Oxford, England: Blackwell Publishers, 1999.

———. *The Journey.* New York: Doubleday, 1999.

———. *The Unknown God.* Grand Rapids, MI: William B. Eerdmans, 1999.

Meyer, F.B. *The Secret of Guidance.* Chicago: Moody Press, 1997.

Miller, Calvin. *Into the Depths of God: Where Eyes See the Invisible, Ears Hear the Inaudible, and Minds Conceive the Inconceivable.* Minneapolis: Bethany House, 2000.

Plantinga, Cornelius. *Not the Way It's Supposed to Be.* Grand Rapids, MI: William B. Eerdmans, 1995.

Schaeffer, Francis A. *The God Who Is There.* Downers Grove, IL: InterVarsity Press, 1968.

———. *True Spirituality.* Wheaton, IL: Tyndale House, 1971.

Stott, John. *The Sermon on the Mount: 12 Studies for Individuals or Groups.* Downers Grove, IL: InterVarsity Press, 1978.

Strohmer, Charles. *The Gospel and the New Spirituality.* Nashville, TN: Thomas Nelson, 1996.

Tozer, A.W. *The Pursuit of God.* Camp Hill, PA: Christian Publications, 1993.

Waller, Ralph, and Benedicta Ward. *An Introduction to Christian Spirituality.* Great Britain: Society for Promoting Christian Knowledge, 1999.

Willard, Dallas. *The Divine Conspiracy: Rediscovering Our Hidden Life in God.* New York: HarperCollins, 1998.

———. *Hearing God: Developing a Conversational Relationship with God.* Downers Grove, IL: InterVarsity Press, 1984.

———. *The Spirit of the Disciplines: Understanding How God Changes Lives.* New York: HarperCollins, 1988.

Yaconelli, Michael. *Dangerous Wonder.* Colorado Springs, CO: NavPress, 1998.

Notes

Spirituality and Relationship

1. Francis Schaeffer, *The God Who Is There* (Downers Grove, IL: InterVarsity Press, 1968), pp. 145-146.

Chapter 1—What Is Spirituality?

1. Clark Pinnock, *Three Keys to Spiritual Renewal* (Minneapolis: Bethany House Publishers, 1985), p. 37.

Chapter 2—Longing

1. Chris Heath, Interview with Brad Pitt, *Rolling Stone,* Oct. 28, 1999, RS #824.

2. C.S. Lewis, "The Weight of Glory" from *They Asked for a Paper* (London: Geoffrey Bles Ltd., 1962), pp. 207-208.

Chapter 3—Belonging

1. As found in Luis Palau, *Healthy Habits for Spiritual Growth* (Grand Rapids, MI: Discovery House, 1994).

2. C.S. Lewis, *Mere Christianity* (New York: Macmillan, 1978), p. 54.

3. William Temple, as quoted by Rowland Croucher. Internet site: <http://www.pastornet.net.au>.

4. A.W. Tozer, *The Pursuit of God* (Camp Hill, PA: Christian Publications, 1993), p. 18.

Chapter 4—Resting

1. Paul Tournier, *Reflections from the Adventure of Living* (New York: Harper and Row, 1965).

Chapter 6—Learning

1. F.B. Meyer, *The Secret of Guidance* (Chicago: Moody Press, 1997), p. 31.

2. John Stott, *Culture and the Bible* (Downers Grove, IL: IVP, 1981), p. 33.

3. See the Westminster Confession of Faith, 1.7-9.

4. Some good additional in-depth resources would be a set of Bible encyclopedias like the *New International Standard Bible Encyclopedia* or *The Illustrated Bible Dictionary.* There are Bible commentaries like the *Expositor's Bible Commentary* or the *Tyndale New Testament Commentaries.* For a closer look at the original language of a passage, there are Hebrew and Greek concordances such as *Strong's Exhaustive Concordance of the Bible* and *Young's Analytical Concordance to the Bible.*

   Other extremely helpful resources are the various on-line Bible study web sites. Some of my favorite web sites are:
   - Biblical Studies Foundation at <http://www.Bible.org>
   - Bible Gateway at <http://bible.gospelcom.net>
   - Blue Letter Bible at <http://www.blueletterbible.org>
   - Christian Classics Ethereal Library at <http://www.ccel.org>

Chapter 7—Praying

1. William Barclay, *The Gospel of Matthew,* vol. 1 (Philadelphia: The Westminster Press, 1975), pp. 199-200.

2. Jon Courson, *Tree of Life Bible Commentary: Matthew,* vol. 1. (Jacksonville, OR: Tree of Life Publishing, 1993).

Chapter 8—Struggling

1. Walter Hooper, *C.S. Lewis: Companion and Guide* (Great Britain: HarperCollins, 1996), p. 265.

Chapter 9—Receiving

1. Here I have adapted a phrase from theologian John Stott.

2. Brennan Manning, *Ruthless Trust* (New York: HarperCollins, 2000), p. 171.

3. C.S. Lewis, "On Forgiveness" from *The Weight of Glory* (New York: Macmillan, 1980).

4. Kim Thomas, *Simplicity: Finding Peace by Uncluttering Your Life* (Nashville, TN: Broadman & Holman, 1999), p. 111.

Chapter 10—Worshiping

1. Calvin Miller, *Into the Depths of God* (Minneapolis: Bethany House, 2000), p. 98.

2. The Westminster Shorter Catechism, source: <http://www.puritansermons.com>.

3. William Temple, as quoted in Warren Wiersbe, *The Integrity Crisis* (Nashville, TN: Thomas Nelson, 1991), p. 119.

Chapter 11—Hearing

1. Robert Benson, *Between the Dreaming and the Coming True* (San Francisco: HarperSanFrancisco, 1997), p. 55.

2. See David Clyde Jones, *Biblical Christian Ethics* (Grand Rapids, MI: Baker Books, 1994), pp. 61-68.

3. William Barclay, *The Plain Man's Book of Prayers* (Allen, TX: Christian Classics, Inc., 1959).

Chapter 12—Becoming

1. F.B. Meyer, *The Secret of Guidance* (Chicago: Moody Press, 1997), p. 12.

2. Richard Foster, as quoted in Edythe Draper, *Draper's Book of Quotations for the Christian World* (Wheaton, IL: Tyndale House, 1992), p. 18.

For more information contact:

Jim Thomas
PO Box 121954
Nashville, TN 37212
E-mail: WatershedStudy@aol.com
Phone: 615-297-8116

Other Good
Harvest House Reading

Can the Real Jesus Still Be Found?
by Sigmund Brouwer

Speaking to young adults facing pain and disappointment, Sigmund reveals Jesus, the man—a young radical who valued ideals over possessions; taught that God is love; was crucified and resurrected; and lives in His people today.

Ice Cream as a Clue to the Meaning of the Universe
by Billy Sprague

Ranging from wildly hilarious to painfully honest, this collection of thought-provoking observations shares glimpses of heaven witnessed every day by focusing on the (sometimes wacky) beauty of relatives, life after tragedy, God's amazing grace, and more.